How to start a business

*Step-By-Step Start from Business Idea and
Business Plan
to Having Your Own Small Business,
Including Home-Based Business Tips, Sole
Proprietorship, LLC, Marketing, Branding,
and More.*

Contents

Introduction

This book is designed to help you take your idea and turn it into a powerful business plan that will generate massive success for years to come. Everything you need to know about starting a business, from the plan to legal structures, to customer experience and outsourcing is all included in this excellent guide. Anything you need to know to succeed will be found within.

Starting a business is an exciting experience. It also requires a lot of time, attention, and support in order to succeed. I assume that since you are reading this book, you are ready to breathe life into your idea and give it whatever it takes to succeed. For that, I congratulate you. Having ambition and drive is the first major necessity in launching a business. Something tells me you have that part covered. So now, let's introduce you to everything else involved in building your business.

If you are ready to learn the ins and outs of running the best business of your dreams, let's begin! Please take your time, as I recognize that this can be a lot of information to take in and there is a lot to do. Make sure to practice healthy business ownership skills now by being realistic about your time and resources and giving yourself the chance to really consume all of the information effectively. This will ensure that you don't miss anything and that you are completely set to run your business! And of course, enjoy!

Part 1: Your Plan

Chapter 1: Building Your Vision

The first step in building any business is having a vision! After all, if you have no idea what it is that you are trying to build, you are going to have a hard time building it. In this chapter, we are going to explore what it takes to build a vision, what you need to consider, and how you can get really clear and expansive on your ideas.

What is a Vision?

A business vision is essentially a plan or idea you come up with to start a business. The majority of people who desire to get into business for themselves already have some form of pre-existing idea of what they want to get into business with. This does not mean that you have the entire basis for the business planned out, but it does mean that you have a general idea of what you want to do.

The birth of a vision can come in any number of ways. Some people are deeply passionate about something and desire to fill their schedule with this particular activity. They therefore want to start a business around it. Others see a need for a certain product or service and decide to create it and take advantage of this opportunity on the market. Furthermore, others may simply know that they want to go into business and so they are looking for a vision to work with.

What is Your Vision?

If you already have a vision, now is a good time to get clear on what your vision is, exactly. The best way to do this is to write it down to get it out on paper. Consider everything that leads you to create this vision and everything that contributes to bringing it to life. For example, if you want to recreate an existing product to sell, explain why you want to do this and highlight how yours is going to be different from anyone else's that already exists.

Your vision is the inspiration that you have for your business. As you go about writing down your vision and the aspects that you already know, be sure to spend some time getting inspired and expanding your view. The more you know about your vision, the easier it will be to test it and turn it into an actionable plan later on.

What If You Don't Have One Yet?

If you don't already have a business vision, now is the time to come up with one. What exactly you end up with will be up to you, but it is important that you choose something that you will genuinely be interested in. Picking a business vision that you have zero interest in will likely result in you losing interest in the business in general. When we don't pursue something that we are interested in or passionate about, we tend not to experience as much success.

That being said, begin exploring your options by considering what you are interested in and passionate about. See what comes up for you and then go from there in researching business ideas that are available to you. The list of things that can be turned into a business is incredibly expansive. There truly is no limit on what can be done.

A great place to start in your research is by going on the internet and researching businesses relating to your passion or interest. Then, go down the list of ideas you find until you come to something that you genuinely care about and are interested in doing. From there, you can go ahead and proceed with developing your vision and turning it into a viable plan.

How Can I Develop my Vision?

Developing your vision will happen a lot more when you are in the process of turning it from a vision into a plan. For now, however, an effective thing to do is sit with the vision and brainstorm. Get really creative with this and take some time considering all areas. Write down any way you could be innovative and evolve your vision into something greater. This will help you immensely when it comes to turning it into a plan and outlining where and why you are going to be most successful.

At this time, there is no need to consider what is "reasonable." Play around with ideas and have an "anything goes" rule for what you come up with and write down. The more you flex your imagination now, the more unique your business idea may become. In many cases, this results in a business owner or an entrepreneur being left with an incredibly innovative idea that sets their business apart from others in a major way. Many business owners even experience massive success as a result!

Chapter 2: Verifying Your Vision

Now that you have your vision and idea down, it is time to begin discovering whether or not it can actually make you money. After all, you do not want to invest your time, energy and resources into launching a business that is not actually going to generate you any income! In this chapter, you are going to discover how you can test your vision and ensure that it is one worth pursuing.

Is the Timing Right?

Timing has a lot to do with whether or not a business will be successful. Many people say "there is nothing better than an idea whose time has come." This is exactly what you need to consider when you are starting your business.

You need to make sure that when you officially hit "launch" on your idea, the world is ready to receive it. For example, many people who went into business in the mid-1990s had massive success in having some level of an online element added into the business. However, the internet was still in its infancy at that time. This means that anyone who was trying to run an exclusively online business would likely fail as there was simply not enough traffic for them to succeed. An exception to this rule would be Amazon, which was an exclusively online company launched by Jeff Bezos in the mid-to-late 1990s, and is now one of the most successful companies in the world.

Still, the majority of companies that tried to operate exclusively online back then did not realize a high rate of return. Unless the owners were willing to pursue it at all costs and ride it out until it became successful, there was little hope for success.

Nowadays, the online element of a business is arguably one of the most important. That is of course, depending on what business you are running. Still, even businesses that are not run online in any way whatsoever are still known to benefit from having an online presence. This is because virtually everyone hangs out online and it is one of the easiest and most cost-effective ways to get directly in front of your audience. If you are not online, you are certainly not taking advantage of one of the most useful tools available to you. This means you are likely not making as much as you could be.

As you can see, timing meant a lot to people who wanted to run an online business. A few started right away and of those, very few actually made it in the long run. For those who had the dream and waited, though, they are now living at the most ideal time to be getting online and launching a business. By waiting until the idea's time had come, they significantly increased their likelihood of success overall.

Are You Willing to Do Whatever It Takes?

As you read in the previous section, the exception to that wait-it-out internet rule, was Jeff Bezos who runs Amazon. This was not because he was lucky or did anything differently. In fact, everything he did essentially had the odds stacked against him. But, because he was willing to pursue it no matter what, he was able to generate a massively successful online company.

The same goes for you! No matter what you are seeking to pursue, you need to ensure that you have what it takes to make it successful. You should be willing to go all in. Business is not known to be easy.

People who want it to be easy are employees, not business owners. Sure, there are many great freedoms and benefits that come with being the owner. It's anything but easy, though, especially in the beginning when you are either completely alone or surrounded by only a limited number of other people sharing your vision.

If you want to know if your idea is going to be successful or not, consider what lengths you are willing to go to in order to actually make it a success. Are you willing to pursue it at nearly all costs? Or are you only doing it because you want to make money and be an entrepreneur? If you are not willing to suffer to some degree to make your business a success, there is a good chance that you will not make it over any of the hurdles you have to face as a business owner. And that's extremely important—especially early on—in the life of your business.

This does not mean that doing business is going to be some massive burden. In fact, it's typically quite the opposite. The majority of business owners will tell you that even though it can be an intense struggle and far more challenging than they ever anticipated, the journey of owning your own business can be deeply rewarding. This is even truer when you pursue something that you are genuinely passionate about.

Are Other People Actually Interested In It?

Finally, if you want to know if your business will take off, consider whether other people will actually be interested in it. As you probably know, a business without customers is no business at all. You need to pay attention to what other people are interested in. This will also help you determine the timing. Going back to the internet business industry: just twenty years ago there was nearly no market there. This doesn't mean that no one was ever going to be interested in shopping online; the time simply had not come and it was not something people were interested in *yet*.

Pay attention to other businesses, and to trends that exist in society. Often, if you listen around you can hear whether or not people would actually be interested in what you have to offer. If the answer is no, you may want to hold on to that idea for a while and let it percolate. Or, you may wish to pursue something more solid and likable by the public in the meantime, letting the other idea sit on the back burner and wait for its time to come.

Chapter 3: From Vision to Action

Turning your vision into an actionable plan requires a few steps. In this chapter, we are going to explore what is needed in order for you to transform your great idea into a business. If you're ready, let's begin!

Research

The first step to turning your vision into an actionable plan is researching. Now that you have a brilliant idea that you have thought out, it is time to create something with it. You want to research everything from the best structure to pursue, to your target audience. You are going to learn more about each of these elements throughout the rest of the book, but for now, you need to research enough to make a viable business plan with. You will learn more about business plans in the next chapter.

Essentially, you want to know everything that you can about your business so that you are able to have a clear idea of what you'll be doing. With diligent research and education, you can ensure that everything you do nurtures and supports your business growth. The more you know, the easier it is for you to take action and build your business.

Make a Timeline

No plan is successful if there is not some kind of timeline in place for you to create success with. You need to break your start-up goal into actionable steps so that you can ensure you're on track. What this will look like exactly will vary from business to business, but ideally, yours will look similar.

Set a date for the following parts of the process, plus any others that you decide will be necessary for starting up your unique business:

- When you want to have your business plan completed by
- When you want to have enough start-up funds for you to begin
- When you want to have your final product/service made by
- When you want to have the structure for sales in place (i.e. rent a storefront, have your website set up, etc.)
- When you want to start market research and testing your products/services
- When you want to begin building the framework of your brand
- When you want to start marketing your brand to your audience
- When you want to officially begin selling to your customers

These are all activities that need to happen in order for you to successfully launch your business with every element in place and ready to go. How long each of these steps will take may vary depending on what you are selling, how your business is structured, and more. This part of the planning stages can take anywhere from three months to a year. Some businesses find themselves continuing to nurture their start-up phase for a little over a year.

The best way to determine how long this will take you and make a reasonable and realistic timeline is to check out Chapters 7 to 9, where we discuss the basics of the different types of businesses. This will help you get a better idea of what to expect. You can also use those chapters to help you determine everything that needs to go on your timeline. Lastly, you might consider doing some internet research on what other companies similar to yours have done, and how long their start-ups took.

Take Action

The final step of having an actionable plan is actually taking action! Once you have your action plan in place, make sure that you are regularly devoting time to it. Set aside a few hours a day, or a few hours a week minimum, to invest in working your way through the timeline. This will ensure that you have plenty of time devoted to getting what you need done so that you can proceed with your start-up.

For many, the early start-up process is where they lose interest and focus and begin to backslide. This can be when finances dwindle, attention or interest begins to fall apart, or you simply don't feel motivated because you are not seeing instant results. Remember, if the idea was not worth this time and attention, it is not one that you should be taking into start-up phases. If it is, then you need to practice discipline now. Get serious, get motivated, and stay on task!

If you find yourself losing motivation, there are many places you can go where you can actually sign up to receive an accountability partner. This is someone who has no impact or involvement in your business, but who supports you and offers words of encouragement as needed to keep you on track. Likewise, you offer the same support and encouragement back to them. This is a great way to stay on track, as well as to expand your options and perception and receive insight from another individual. Many people develop "business buddies" this way, which can be invaluable to a start-up. If you find you are struggling to stay motivated, looking for an accountability partner may just help.

Alternatively, you might consider looking for a mentor. Business mentors are individuals who have launched a business similar to yours, or who have a company that resembles what you want your company to look like. Your mentor should carry the same values and morals as you do and should have teachable skills that are directly related to the type of business you want to run for yourself. Having a knowledgeable and skilled mentor can help you greatly when it comes to having your questions answered, receiving support in taking action, or otherwise getting through those early stages of starting your own business.

Support, in general, is invaluable. If you find that you need that extra encouragement or support, know that there are many options available to you as a start-up business owner. Make sure that you stay honest with yourself and that if you feel like you do need help, be sure you reach out and get some.

Chapter 4: Building a Business Plan

Now that you have your actionable plan in place, you'll want to start building your business plan! Your business plan is typically made at the same time as you are conducting research. It's essentially a well-prepared research paper that validates the likelihood of your business succeeding and helps ensure that you are prepared for the next steps in business. Business plans tend to outline the five-year objective of the business. You will learn more about each section of the business plan below, and what you need to do in order to complete it.

Why You Need a Proper Business Plan

A business plan serves many purposes in a business. The two primary purposes it serves: as a guide to keep the business on track, and as a tool to receive investors should they be needed.

For keeping the business on track, the business plan helps to identify goals. It also helps to identify what needs to be done in order for success to be achieved. It can be used by the business owner as well as managers and other individuals in charge within the company to keep everyone on track. The business plan can help ensure that every move the business makes and every step that is taken contributes to the success plan of the business. Without it, most businesses will operate with no clear goals in mind, nor on-brand, relevant and effective steps to succeed.

As a financial tool, your plan shows potential investors what your numbers look like, what your success strategy is, and why you are worthy of investment. It is used as proof that you have done your research and that you are worth taking the gamble on. When you have completed it effectively, you can use it to encourage investors to invest in your company, allowing you to access start-up funds, or investments to get you past the start-up stage.

Executive Summary

The first part of the business plan you need to develop is the executive summary. This summary will highlight the key points in your business plan. It needs to be short and concise and focused on the purpose of the plan. Many people believe this is the most important part of the plan because it is used to catch people's attention, so make sure it is both clear and interesting.

In this section you want to include:

- Highlights of each of the other sections.
- A brief explanation of your business

The executive summary should be very clear, short and concise. This may be up to two pages long but should be no longer than that. Keep in mind that even though this is going to be the first section in your business plan, it should be the last one that you write. This will ensure that you are writing it with reference to what is actually *in* your business plan. Writing it last will keep it clear and accurate, and prevent you from having to redo it at any given time.

Business Strategy

The business strategy needs to be fairly brief, but clear in describing the purpose and intent of your business. The easiest way to write this section is to include the following elements within it:

Introduction

This will be the shortest part of the section. The entire purpose of it is to introduce your business idea, offer a brief history of your business (i.e. are you a concept, young business, or already established?), explain the purpose of your business, and offer a description of products and services. You should also take a moment to explain the legal structure of your business, as this is an important element of what your business actually is, especially to potential investors or anyone else who may be interested in seeing your business plan.

Current Position

This is your opportunity to let readers know what stage you are at in your business. Let them know the life stage you are in, what industry you are in, what state that industry is in (contracting, stable, or growing) and your achievements to date.

Competitive Advantage

Your readers will be curious to know why you are an eligible competitor against the other businesses that currently exist within your industry. This is your opportunity to explain why you have a competitive advantage, who your competitors are, and how your business model contributes to your competitiveness.

Growth Plan

Having a solid growth plan is important. This is your opportunity to show your readers where you intend to be, and when. You should include a growth timeline here that expresses where you plan to be in one year, three years, and five years. You also want to include milestones, which are essentially your objectives and how you can tell that you are achieving them. Lastly, include your goals. These will include the goals you have right away within the coming year and within your 3-5-year range. Including all of this information will ensure that you and anyone else reading this business plan has a clear sense of your direction, which makes it a lot easier to understand where you are going and what your intentions are.

Marketing Strategy

Including a marketing strategy ensures that you are clear on what you are doing to actually get your products or services to market. In this section, you are going to highlight these strategies and explain why they work.

Your marketing strategy should consist of the four "P"s that are included in any strong marketing recipe. These include product, price, place, and promotion. You can learn more about each respective one below.

Product

Begin by explaining why your product or service is needed in the first place. What need are you meeting for your target audience? How is your product meeting this need? You should also take a moment to explain why your product or service is competitive against others that already exist in the market.

Price

Take a moment to explain what price point you have your product or service at, and why you have chosen this one. This doesn't need to be long, but providing a strong statement as to why you have chosen this will ensure that you and anyone else reading your business plan understands that thought has gone into your pricing structure.

Place

This is your opportunity to express how you are getting your products to the market. Where are you selling them? Are they going in a storefront? Are you selling them online, or through infomercials? Explain what you are doing to get your products to the market, and be sure to explain why this is the most efficient method available to you. Give your reader an idea as to why you have chosen this route.

Promotion

Lastly, explain how you are going to create connections and relationships with your target market. What will you do that will have people paying attention to you, your brand, and your product? How are you going to ensure that people hear about you and that they are actively interested in purchasing what you have to offer? This is where your marketing materials and content comes into play. Be sure to give it some thought, as this is the actual process of connecting with potential customers and you want to make sure you are doing that effectively!

Operational Plan

This section needs to give a general overview of how you are going to operate your day-to-day operations in your business over a prolonged period of time. This should include what you are currently doing, as well as what you project that you will need to be doing in 3-5 years' time to ensure that you stay up-to-date with operational requirements.

The things that should be included in this section include day-to-day operations, facility requirements, management information systems and information technology requirements. This means that you ensure that everyone understands what you are currently doing as well as what you project you'll be doing to keep your business operating.

Here is what you need to include for each subject:

Day-to-Day Operations

Here, you want to make sure that your reader has a general sense of what is required to operate your business on a daily basis. Include information such as your hours of operation, whether or not your business is seasonal, who supplies your business and what their credit terms are, and anything else relevant to your day-to-day operations.

Facility Requirements

Here, you need to identify what you need in order of physical space. If you require a physical landmark for your business, be specific about what size and location you need to be in now, and what you project you will need to be in when you reach your 3-5 year milestone. If you are currently holding any lease agreements or supplier quotations, you will want to include this information in your appendix later on and cite it here. If there are any special requirements you have, or licensing specifics, include this in your appendix as well.

Management Information Systems

Any business that has customers, needs a strategy for management. Your management information systems include how you are managing customers and accounts, as well as how you are managing stock if you have any. In this section, include any information relevant to how you are managing this information. If you have quality control measures, this should be included here as well.

Information Technology (IT) Requirements

If you have any IT systems you are using for your business, which virtually every business does, you want to include it now. It is important to indicate here if you are using a consultant or if you have an IT support service that you use. You should also include outlines to any planned developments you have in your IT department.

Strengths, Weaknesses, Opportunities and Threats Analysis

The strengths, weaknesses, opportunities and threats analysis is often known as the SWOT analysis in business. This analysis is essential when you are planning a business, as it provides your potential investors with the assurance that you are being realistic about these four key elements.

Even if you do not plan in asking for financial support right now, having the SWOT analysis is still an important part of completing your business plan. It allows you to get realistic with what you are up against and how you can secure your success in the business world.

When you have a proper SWOT analysis, you are better able to make decisions for your business and plans for its future. It becomes easier for you to anticipate any problems that may arise and proactively face them. It also helps ensure that you take advantage of any opportunities that align with your growth, and see that your business stays healthy and thriving.

You should review your SWOT analysis on a regular basis (at least every three months) to ensure that it remains accurate and focuses on where you can grow in your business. It also helps hedge you against potential risks due to threats and weaknesses.

Human Resources Plan

Businesses typically require some form of employee structure. The only instance where this may not be true is if you are running a sole proprietorship. At that point, you may still want to consider completing this section, as you can include valuable information as to who, when, and how you intend to hire people when it comes to scaling your business in the future.

In the meantime, your human resources plan needs to discuss short-term and long-term plans when it comes to recruiting, training, and retaining employees. What should be included in this section is a brief layout or chart of the business and where different employees fit in. This includes who is doing what, what their position entails, the skills that are required for each position, how you are training your employees, and anything else that may be relevant to your employee hiring structure. For example, if there are any gaps in your team, explain why, and if you need a budget for training your employees to explain what that is.

This section is actually essential when it comes to potential investors, but is also a great tool for organizing your business. It is important that you take advantage of it and structure it accordingly. Take the time to ensure that whoever is reading your business plan understands that you have taken great care and interest in ensuring that your business is being scaled in a way that is reasonable, realistic, and effective toward your end goals for growth.

Social Responsibility Strategy

A part of running a good business is having good environmental and social practices incorporated into your business. Not only does this give you a great competitive advantage, but it also boosts the reputation and goodwill toward your business. Pay attention to ethical values surrounding your business and use this section to highlight how your company is going to uphold its social responsibility. This should include those surrounding both the community and the environment.

Some information you can include in this section would be:

- Environmental initiatives and policies your company has
- How you are contributing to your community (current as well as in the future)
- Any relevant certifications you have contributing to this (i.e. organic certification, fair-trade certification, etc.)
- Any environmental programs you may become involved in to improve your business
- Where your corporate social responsibility fits in

E-Business Strategy

These days, the internet is an essential tool for virtually everyone, especially businesses. It is a good idea to include some information regarding what your online strategy is for your business. Use this section as an opportunity to outline how you intend to use the technology of the internet to further reach, and interact with your customers, manage and scale your business, and reduce costs that you incur in running it.

You can include information in this section such as:

- Any e-commerce activities you are going to be engaging in (how you sell your products and/or services on the internet)
- Your website and how you intend to develop it to be effective for customer use
- Any hardware or software requirements you have to manage and scale your business online
- The relationships you have with outsourced specialists who are helping maintain this side of your business

If you are using the internet as a means to reduce costs and save money in your business, it may be a good idea to highlight this factor in this section. Doing so will ensure that if you are seeking investors, they see that you are paying attention to how you can reduce costs effectively in your business.

Financial Forecasts and Other Information

Every business plan needs some information regarding cash flow and financial forecasts. This section is going to give you space to discuss how your business plan turns into a bottom line. This will include your current standings, as well as your forecast for the next 3-5 years in business. It is important, however, to include more expansive detail in the first 12 months outlined in this section, as this is your immediate future and will provide proof for what you have forecast in your long-term future.

It is important that you think about your plan objectively when it comes to finances, staying clear on what your optimistic, pessimistic and realistic numbers could be. This ensures that you know what to expect moving forward. It also means that, should you choose to seek financing, you have considered all views and you know how to explain your financial situation to anyone with any perspective.

In this section, you need to include the following:

- Statements for cash flow – this includes what your cash flow looks like for the first 12-18 months in your business. If you have already been in business for some time, you can use your existing cash flow charts and build from there. If you have not, you will need to do research and see what the most probable and realistic circumstance is and go from there. This needs to include working capital, sales, and salaries.
- Forecast for profits and losses – make sure you are clear on how much you believe you will make, as well as how much you will lose given the cost of running your business. Again, be realistic and clear here to avoid sounding over-optimistic and unrealistic to potential investors.
- Sales forecast – this is specifically how much you intend to sell. In this section, discuss what your revenue will look like and why.

As you are writing this section, you need to consider what your purpose for your business plan is. If you are seeking investors, consider what you need from them and include a "request statement" here. You also need to consider what you are going to do to ensure the security of your investors, how you plan to repay them, and how many different sources of revenue and income you are earning from your business to repay them as quickly as possible.

Business Exit Strategy

Every business needs an exit strategy. While you likely don't want to be considering the demise of your business, it is something that could happen and having a proper exit strategy will ensure that everything is in place should you come to this point in the future. This is good for yourself, but also for your investors, should you have any.

An exit strategy allows you to determine how you know when to exit the business, and what you are going to do in order to leave it behind. If you plan on passing this business on to your children, then you need to incorporate *your* exit strategy, too. For example, the amount of time it will take you to effectively train them to take over.

To prepare a strong exit strategy, include the following information in this section:

- When am I going to leave my business?
- What do I plan on doing with my business when I do (i.e. sell it, pass it on to family, close it and liquidate its assets, etc.)?
- What will determine the value of the business?
- After exiting my business, how much money do I need to lead a comfortable life?

Appendix

The final section you need to incorporate in your business plan is your appendix. Here, you want to include all information that is relevant to your business. For example, if you cited employees in your business, use this as a place to include resumes. You can also include lease agreements, licensing papers, patents, and anything else relevant to your business here.

This is essentially the point where you include the "in-depth" information, should anyone desire to see it when they are looking over your business plan. This keeps it organized and complete, and also ensures that if you approach any investors, that they have access to all of the information they need right away. Including this shows that you are organized and prepared, which is important in any business venture and move.

Part Two: Your Structure

Chapter 5: What Structures Are Available?

There are many different structures that are used to operate businesses. These structures describe how the business is run, including the model of the business itself. They also includes information about how each structure is likely to grow, what you can do to scale, and more.

It is important that you pick the right structure for your business. Not only will this help with the model of your business, but it also contributes to the legality factor. Below, you will find information about all of the different legal structures you may consider when it comes to developing and running your business.

Sole Proprietorship

A sole proprietorship is the type of structure that is used by individuals or married couples who are in business alone. These tend to be the most commonly developed business structures, as they are simple to create and operate. There are fewer legal controls in these structures in general, which allows greater flexibility when it comes to operation. There are also fewer taxes involved. The primary downside to this structure is that you carry all liability personally.

Some businesses, typically sole proprietorship businesses, may be run as what is known as a "home business." This means that the business is run from the individual's home. Businesses like this have a broad range in what activities are fulfilled. They also still have a certain amount of legal requirements to ensure that protection standards are met. If you are running a home business online, the number of legal requirements you have are low, if any. If you are running a home business where clients will be coming into your home for any reason, you need to look into your local legal requirements. Most require you to have a business/home inspection done, have your space licensed, and purchase insurance to protect your clients and yourself. Certain requirements will likely need to be met in order to ensure the safety of the general public.

General Partnership

General partnerships include two or more partners together who have agreed to each contribute to the business. They typically contribute through money, labor, or their skills. The two or more individuals are typically not in a marital relationship when they are in a general partnership legal structure. In this structure, each person is included in profits, losses, and general management over the business itself. They typically carry equal partnership rights, meaning they are equally able to receive benefits, as well as to receive liability for the business. Typically, general partnerships are drafted up with a formal partnership agreement that is written as a contract between the partners.

Limited Partnership

Limited partnerships are like general partnerships, except that one or more of the partners involved in the structure are considered to be limited. This means that the general partners are responsible for managing the business itself and are each involved in sharing in the profits and losses that the business realizes. Limited partners will

---

share in the profits, but will be protected against any losses based on how much they have invested in the company. A limited partner will not typically become involved in day-to-day operations for the business. These structures are generally required by law to be filed with your local government.

Limited Liability Partnership (LLP)

Most professionals use this structure. It is essentially the same as a general partnership, except that partners will not have personal liability should another partner be negligent in their business. These are really common structures in lawyers and accountant offices, where the individuals are typically at higher risk of negligence and partners want to be protected from someone else's potential mistakes.

Limited Liability Limited Partnership (LLLP)

This limited liability limited partnership is typically the exact same as a limited liability partnership, except there are statements in the certificate that indicate the limited partnership. These structures are also known to be useful in protecting general partners as well as limited partners.

Corporation

Corporations carry a far more complex system compared to sole proprietorships or partnerships. Corporations become their own independent identity outside of the individual or partners, and therefore the corporation carries its own privileges, rights, and liabilities. There are typically many tax and financial benefits that come with running a corporation. However, they may be offset by other things that business owners need to consider, such as the increased cost of licensing fees, or the decreased amount of personal control that the individual has over their company.

Non-Profit Corporation

A corporation that registers as a non-profit, is one that is structured exactly like a corporation. However, the goal is more in the interest of the business than in the profit it can create. These are typically used to serve public interest, such as charities or otherwise. If you run a non-profit corporation that also intends to raise donations from public donors, you will likely need to register for a Charity Program as per your local laws. This will provide you with a charity number, legitimizing your charity and further protecting both yourself and your donors and [customers] from potential fraud.

Limited Liability Company (LLC)

Limited liability companies are comprised of one or more individuals. These companies include a special written agreement that details the organization of the LLC, assigns interests, includes any provisions for management, and how profits and losses are distributed. A company that registers as an LLC is generally capable of carrying out any for-profit business activities, other than banking or insurance.

Chapter 6: Choosing Your Structure

Hearing how many different structures exist can be daunting. It is important that you choose the proper structure for your business. This ensures that you are able to run it accordingly, that it is legally structured in a way which protects you and your partners (if applicable) to the maximum extent, and that the structure serves the best interests of your company.

Choosing what structure you need is not as hard as it may seem. In fact, it truly varies from person to person, and situation to situation. This is especially true in the circumstances of small businesses or start-ups that are intended to launch into the small business world.

In some cases, talking to an attorney may be the best strategy for you to discover what the best structure for your unique business will be. This ensures that your legal interests are covered and that you understand what the laws for your local area are. Remember, they do vary from place to place, meaning that you need to ensure that you are clear on what is applicable to you when it comes to structuring your business. This will keep you, your business, and your clients safe.

Outside of the idea of talking to an attorney to get access to the best information possible, you can also consider the following. Answering the questions below will give you an idea of where you are at in your business.

How many individuals are currently involved in running your business?

If the answer is just you, or just you and your spouse, you might want to consider running a sole proprietorship. This is one of the easiest structures to form and has the ability to give you flexibility in how you run your business. If you want to limit your personal liability, you might consider registering as a Limited Liability Company.

If the answer is you and other individuals, consider looking into starting a partnership. This will enable you all to be legally accounted for and protected in your business. Be sure to work with an attorney to get this set up in the best structure for each of you. This will determine what type of partnership will best suit the needs of your business, and the partners involved.

If you are looking to build a business with partners and with multiple employees, you might consider starting a corporation. This allows the business to become its own entity and be supported legally in a way that mitigates any legal liability from each individual involved in running the company.

How much liability are you willing to take on?

Liability equals risk. If you are held personally liable for anything, this means you could potentially stand to lose a lot. In a situation such as a sole proprietorship, for example, you are on the line with unlimited liability. This means should anything tragic happen, you are held personally responsible and have to face any and all consequences as a result.

If you are running a company where the liability is seemingly low or you are protected, you might consider maintaining your status as a sole proprietorship. If you are a partnership, you might consider becoming limited liability partners to prevent any of you from being held responsible for the other's mistakes. Or, you might consider becoming limited liability partners to protect you to the max against any mistakes in the business in general.

Alternatively, if you don't want to hold any responsibility and you have enough individuals to form the structure, you might consider starting a corporation. This takes the personal liability load off everyone involved and ensures that you are all protected in the event of a tragic accident. In this circumstance, the corporation would take all of the risks and you, personally, would take none. This means that the corporation could lose everything, but you are likely going to remain safe (depending on the details of the circumstance).

What legal structure best serves your business?

Of course, you need to think about your business goals and objectives. Naturally, certain structures will serve specific goals that you may desire to achieve. For example, if you are looking to start a charity, you will likely want to register as a non-profit corporation. Alternatively, if you are starting a business on your own, you may want to start a sole proprietorship. That is unless you want to limit your risk, then you might consider a limited liability company. If you were going into business by yourself, for example, you would not want to enter into any form of partnership agreement, as it would not hold up for you.

Ensuring that you choose the structure which is going to best serve your business now and in the future is important. While you can generally amend what you initially choose, it tends to be easiest to start off in the way that is going to serve your future goals the best. That way you do not have to incur expensive legal fees later on to advance to where you desire to go.

Once you have considered these questions, you will likely have a strong idea of what legal structure will best serve your business. If not, again, going to speak with a business attorney may be your best opportunity to ensure that you are structured the proper way. It is essential that you choose the proper structure, as this will protect you and set you up for success in the future of your business.

Chapter 7: Home Business Basics

Running a home-based business is one of the most popular types of entrepreneurship at this time. More and more people are joining home-based business opportunities, or creating their own opportunities and using their home as the "head office" of their business.

If this is the structure you are looking into, it is important to ensure that you understand what this entails and how it affects you as a business owner. There are many legal considerations when you are putting together a home-based business. This includes running your business with a direct sales, multi-level marketing, or network marketing structure. Ensuring that your legal responsibilities are met and that you understand your requirements to operate a sound business are important.

Here is what you should consider if you are starting a home-based business:

Pick the Right Structure

As we have just discussed, picking the right structure for your home-based business is important. The majority of home-based businesses are run as a sole proprietorship. However, you might consider running yours as a limited liability company to protect the safety of yourself and your family in the event of a tragic legal battle.

Get Your Business License

Your local government will more than likely require you to have a business license. These licenses do not regulate your business, but instead, keep your business legally registered. The best way to tell if you will need a business license is to answer this question: will you need to file taxes for the income you are making? If the answer is yes, you need a business license.

If Necessary, Obtain an Occupational License

Depending on what you are doing, you might need to acquire an occupational license. Certain careers are more restricted than others, and it is important that you are operating with the correct licenses. For example, if you are providing childcare for other people's children, you will need an occupational license. To discover whether your occupation requires an occupational license or not, contact your local governing body. They will have the most accurate answers. It is important that you receive accurate information regarding this, as you do not want to be without a license and later find out one is required for your occupation.

Set Up Your Accounts with Sales Tax Agencies

Virtually all businesses that sell products and/or services are required to pay taxes on their sales. You want to make sure that you get these accounts set up right away. Using these numbers will ensure that you receive the appropriate amount of tax from each sale. You will collect this tax and then pay it to the appropriate governing body.

If you are required to tax the products or services you are offering, you may also need to acquire a "seller's permit," "resale license," or "certificate of authority" depending on what you are offering and what your local legal requirements are.

Protect Your Business Name

It is essential that you have your business name protected. Unless your business name is literally your own name, you will need to check into it to see if it is legally protected yet or not. If not, you will want to purchase the rights to the name. This includes if you are using a name such as "[your name] and associates." Even just adding additional words to your name may result in legal considerations, so marking your name as your trade name is important.

Consider Your Zoning Restrictions

Because you are running your business from your home, you need to consider the restrictions that may exist for you. Some homeowner associations, strata properties, and municipal zones are not eligible for home business ownership. Ensuring that you are legally entitled to run your business as per your zone, homeowner's association, and strata rules is important. This ensures that you are not in violation of any legally governing documents that may deem your business illegally zoned or ineligible to operate in its current location. It is best to consider this *before* you start, rather than to start and later realize you are not legally allowed to!

Direct Sales Specifics

Lastly, if you are operating as a sales consultant for a direct sales, multi-level marketing, or network marketing company, it is essential that you read the fine print in the legal documents you agreed to upon joining your chosen company. Ensure that you remain within your legal obligations, rights, and restrictions as per the contract you have signed. This will protect you against potentially becoming liable for a mistake you make that could be outside of your agreement.

Chapter 8: Sole Proprietorship Basics

Sole proprietorships are the most common form of small business that exists to date. These are one of the simplest forms to create and run, and therefore they are highly popular in the small business industry. Chances are if you have already launched your business, this is the structure under which you are presently running.

It is important that you know how to run your sole proprietorship properly, so in this chapter, we are going to explore how you can educate yourself on this business structure and understand what it means for you. This will give you an idea of everything that you need to do to run your business effectively, within your legal obligations, and otherwise. It will also help you determine whether you want to remain operating as a sole proprietorship, or switch to operating a limited liability company or other choice.

Legal Structure of a Sole Proprietorship

When it comes to legal structures, sole proprietorships are one of the easiest to form, operate, and understand. They also tend to be one of the riskiest. As a sole proprietor, you agree to do business as yourself. This means that you are personally holding yourself liable for any mistakes or mishaps that happen in your business. Your business is not a legal entity; it is merely a way of legally identifying that you operate a business.

You can operate under the name of yourself if you run a sole proprietorship, or you can create a trade name to operate under. A trade name is a business name that is owned by a sole proprietor. These trade names do not create legal entities that are separate from the owner. Instead, they simply identify the name of the business. This still identifies you as the owner, operator, and liable party.

Sole proprietors use their own name and/or trade names to secure licenses. At that point, they are ready to operate their business legally.

How to Form a Sole Proprietorship

Forming a sole proprietorship is generally as easy as declaring you are in business and then operating your business. Legally, you may need to acquire local licenses to qualify your business. However, there is not a lot else to do. No legal contracts, agreements, or other documents legitimize the business since you are in business by yourself. No formal filing is legally required if you are going to form a sole proprietorship. Instead, this status is automatic the moment you choose to engage in business activities on your own.

Disadvantages to Sole Proprietorships

Some disadvantages that you are sure to face as a sole proprietor includes the most common: the fact that you are personally unlimitedly liable for the debts, liabilities, and losses that are incurred by your business. This means that should anything potentially go wrong, you are going to be held personally responsible, and you may lose all that you own as a result of this.

Another disadvantage is that you cannot approach potential investors to raise capital. You may be able to take out a business loan from the bank, but you will not be able to engage in investor relationships. This is because there are no ways to sell shares in a business that does not have shares to be sold.

Lastly, if the owner of the sole proprietorship passes away or otherwise becomes incapable of running their business, the business will likely end as well. Sole proprietorships do not carry or retain value in the same way that incorporated businesses do. Therefore they cannot be traded, passed down, or sold. They are strictly held as business operations by the owner, and that is it.

Advantages to Sole Proprietorships

Despite the fact that there are heavy risks and that your business will not carry value on its own, sole proprietorships do have many advantages that they carry. These include things such as the fact that a sole proprietorship can be instantly established with minimal expenses and no filing requirements. As well, there are little if any ongoing formalities that are required with sole proprietorships. Whereas larger legal structures regularly have to vote on things, work together on coming to decisions, and otherwise consult each other on business activities, sole proprietorships can run on their own and do their own thing. This makes it extremely easy to run your business your way, in a flexible manner.

Another reason is that, if you choose you do not want to, sole proprietors don't have to pay unemployment taxes for themselves. They do still have to pay for their employees should they hire any, however.

Lastly, you can freely mix any business and personal assets you have. Therefore, if you purchase a new car, it can be used for both business and personal purposes interchangeably with no legal considerations to be made. This goes for many different assets. Even though this does carry risk in the liability department, it also makes it really easy for you to operate a business fluidly alongside your lifestyle.

Tax Considerations

There are some tax considerations to think about when it comes to running a sole proprietorship. Because you and your business share a single identity, the taxes you pay are extremely simple. Rather than having to file multiple tax reports, you can simply fill out the personal income report. The page you fill out is simply a self-employment report. This is an extremely simple report to fill out, and it makes filing your taxes incredibly easy. As well, you will not owe any personal unemployment tax because you are not required to pay this as a sole proprietor. (You are, however, required to pay the unemployment tax of your employees.)

Legal Implications

One thing you really need to consider when it comes to running a sole proprietorship is your legal implications. For example, if you are sued, you are being personally sued since you are not separate from your business. This means that your own assets can be held for any implications you may encounter.

For instance: say you take out a loan so you can afford to run your business. Then, for some reason, you default on the loan and are unable to repay it. Your own personal assets such as your home or car could be used as collateral to repay the loan. This can result in personal losses because of a loss to your business.

Another circumstance to consider—even though it can be a challenging one—is a sudden tragic event. For example, say as a result of an accident within your business, someone is injured or killed. You would be held personally responsible for this. This means any legal consequences that are served as a result of this experience would be given directly to you, and not mitigated by your company.

As a sole proprietor, your company can quickly become a legal nightmare for you if you are not careful. The owner is consistently held personally responsible, even if the mistake is on the shoulders of one of the employees. For that reason, it may be ideal to consider choosing a more supported structure, such as a limited liability company, where you can continue to be the single owner of the company, but your legal liability is not as risky compared to sole proprietorships.

Chapter 9: Partnership and LLC Basics

When you choose to go into a more legal structure with your business, the most commonly chosen routes are partnerships and LLCs. In this chapter, we are going to explore the differences between these two structures, and why you might consider them.

LLC as an Individual

Since operating an LLC as an individual is so much different than operating it with a partner, let's take a moment to discuss this option. Running an LLC on your own essentially means that you are running a company similar to that of a sole proprietorship, but the legal structure is quite different. In an LLC, you are operating as a part of a legally recognized company. Your structure limits your liability but also means that you are legally obligated to fulfill certain requirements.

For example, the licensing and certifications you must acquire are quite different. Additionally, your LLC could be subjected to different financial structures. Lastly, when you run an LLC, you have to pay yourself from your business account. Unlike in a sole proprietorship where you are paid directly, individuals will pay your company and then you are paid out of those funds.

If you choose to transition your sole proprietorship into an LLC, it is important that you do so with the assistance of a business attorney.

This will ensure that you are clearly aware of all of your local legal obligations, as well as anything that you may need to know in order to run your business legally and effectively.

LLC vs Partnership

Although the process of forming an LLC and partnerships is similar, there are clear differences between the two.

LLCs are formed in specific localities and are required to file articles of organization with their government. LLC owners are referred to as "members," and function under what is called an operating agreement. The operating agreement defines the percentage of the business owned by each member, as well as any other questions that are typically based on "what if" scenarios.

Partnerships are businesses that are owned by two or more individuals which are legally identified as partners. Like an LLC, you register your partnership with your local government. Which partnership structure you choose will heavily depend on how it varies from the LLC structure, but essentially the partners each become "stockholders" in the company. There is no stock to sell to potential investors, however, this is the easiest way to explain the division of the company between the partners. The percentage owned by each partner may vary and will be outlined in the partnership agreement.

Each partner involved in a partnership becomes personally responsible for their respective share of the profits and losses based on the amount of the company they own. So, for example, if each partner owns 25% of the company and the company is sued, each partner is liable for 25% of the final result.

The biggest difference between an LLC and partnership comes down to liability. In a general partnership, for example, each partner is personally liable. In a limited partnership, limited liability partnership, or limited liability limited partnership, as well as in limited liability companies, the amount of liability held by each individual involved in the company varies depending upon the structure chosen.

Choosing Your Partner

When going into business, it is essential that you choose a partner whom you will enjoy working with and whom you will be able to work with for a long period of time. Going into business with someone can put a lot of stress and strain on a relationship, so choosing to do so with someone whom you can trust, who is reliable, and who is effective at communicating with you, is going to be important. However, there are many other things that you need to consider when it comes to starting a business together.

When you transition from having an idea with someone to actually starting a business with them, there are some more things that you need to consider. This will help you truly determine whether they are going to be worth going into business with or not. While the decision is ultimately up to you and technically nothing legally disqualifies a partner, you do want to make sure that *you* take appropriate action in protecting yourself.

Here are some things to consider when choosing a business partner:

Decide If You Actually Need a Partner

Before you pick a partner, it is a good idea to decide if you actually need one in the first place. Signing a partner does come with a great deal of responsibility and additional legal obligations in your business. You need to be certain that having a partner makes sense. Going into business on your own can have benefits, but so can going into business with a partner. For that reason, you need to consider the reality of your unique circumstance. If you feel that having a partner is the best route to go, then carry on reading this chapter! If not, you may wish to revisit the previous chapter and learn about running a sole proprietorship.

Do you trust this person?

Working with someone whom you cannot trust will only lead to greater struggles in the future. Remember, businesses with a partnership have legally binding agreements. Do you really want to be in a legally binding agreement with this person? Consider it carefully.

Are you friends?

Being friends with your partner can be both a blessing and a curse. First off, being friends with someone means that the chemistry is already there. You know that you enjoy their company and that they enjoy yours, and that you both get along well. You likely also have a good idea as to how you handle conflict in general, as well as with each other. And, because you already know this person, you can get a pretty strong gauge on whether or not they are reliable enough to go into business with.

However, you also need to consider how being friends could complicate things. Going into business only because you are friends can be edging toward dangerous waters. Consider the personal problems your friend has and how this may implicate the business. While they may be a great friend, someone with a poor ability to manage their finances, minimal discipline, and a lack of professionalism could result in you going into partnership with a friend who is not reliable. You also need to make sure that you share the same values and goals in business. Lastly, make sure that they take on responsibility and that they do so in a way that aligns with how you do. Clashing personality types between friends can lead to complications in a business, as well as the potential loss of a friend. This can be a lot to lose.

The same should be considered when it comes to family members. Truly take the time to consider how this relationship could both benefit and implicate your business, and determine whether or not you think you can successfully run your business with this person.

Be objective and realistic. This will ensure that you protect yourself against potential risks to the best of your ability.

Can You Do A Trial Run?

If you can, try doing a trial run with your potential partner. Consider doing something work-related for a short period of time, perhaps working together on a nonprofit cause or something else. Having both of you in a work-related environment at the same time, handling and facing challenges together is a great way to see how well you both work together. This gives you the opportunity to see how they react in challenging situations, what their experiences are, how their strengths complement yours, or how they are as a partner in general. Doing this can give you a really clear example of what it would be like to work together, potentially making it easier to make your final decision.

Consider This: Partner, Employee, or Consultant?

If you are already running a business and you are considering bringing someone in as a partner, consider your motives. Are you bringing them in as a partner because you cannot afford to hire them? Or are you bringing them in because you genuinely believe that they can benefit your company? Take your time and hire someone as a consultant if you cannot afford to hire them as an employee, and have them work with you for a short period of time. It is better to hire someone than it is to give away part of your company in a partnership, only to find out that the partner does not fit with your company despite their qualifications in business.

Consider Your Varied Strengths

When you partner with someone, it is always a good idea to consider partnering with someone who has different strengths then you do. This means that you have varied strengths across the board. As a team, this gives you a much higher chance of winning in business. Rather than having an excessive amount of strength (and potentially clashing hard in certain areas,) you can distribute your strength across the board and each carries the company in a unique way.

Balance the Responsibilities

It is important that you agree immediately upfront on how the responsibilities will be balanced between partners. If you cannot agree, then the partnership may not be ideal. Being able to agree on how responsibility should be distributed and each taking ownership of their responsibilities is important. You do not want to have one partner unknowingly carrying more responsibility because one has decided not to. This can result in resentment and can quickly unravel any partnership.

Consider Money

In partnerships, money can be a major problem between partners. It will virtually always come up in one way or another, so it is best to be prepared for this early on. Agree from the very beginning how funds will be used, how they will be raised, and how profits will be distributed. This ensures that the expectations are clearly defined and no one can later come back and feel as though they have been ripped off, lied to, or otherwise taken advantage of.

Determine Valuation and Contracts

It is important to determine how you will come up with the valuation of your company early on so that, should a partner choose to leave, you are both clear on how the company is valued. As well, you should have any necessary contracts in place, such as buy/sell agreements, to ensure that each party knows exactly what will occur should they decide to sell their part of the company.

Choosing Your Partnership Structure

Once you have determined if your partner is the right fit for you, it is time to determine your legal structure. As you know, there are many legal structures you can consider. The best way to determine your legal structure in a partnership is to go back to Chapter 5 and look at the different types of structures that exist. Then, you should speak with a business attorney about which structure would best suit your mutual interests and needs in business.

When you are choosing your partnership structure, it will largely depend on how much liability you are willing to take on, what the future of your company looks like, what industry you are in, and other aspects. Having the support of a legally trained and educated business attorney can ensure that you and your partner are well-represented and that all of the minor details are ironed out.

To Last Long, Start Out Strong

Lastly, if you want to have a strong partnership that is successful in the long run, you need to think about all of the legal responsibilities, obligations, and considerations early on. Starting out with clear expectations, proper contracts and agreements signed, and other legal considerations dealt with right away can result in all of the partners being properly represented throughout the life of the business.

When you have proper contracts and agreements in place, it ensures that everyone knows what is expected of them and how the business is structured. This means that if anyone ever wants to leave the partnership, they know how to do so and what is expected of them. Additionally, if anything were to ever happen where one partner wronged the partnership or wound up in legal trouble, having your structure and agreements in place early on can protect other partners from this ordeal.

Starting out strong with all of your legal bases covered is essential to ensure that there are no troubles endured later on in your business. It may seem somewhat uncomfortable to talk about these dealings, especially if you are friends or family with this person and want to put it on a handshake or good-faith level, but it is essential. Keeping everyone protected and well-represented is the best way to ensure that everyone within the partnership is legally protected and cared for in the long run. This can also protect relationships and prevent disputes that may arise from miscommunication or misrepresentation on the legal and official front.

Part Three: Funding

Chapter 10: Types of Funding Available

Starting up a business requires start-up funds. If you have your own savings prepared for your venture, you likely will not need any funds for a while. Still, it is important to know what is available to you in case this becomes something you need to take advantage of in the future.

There are many routes you can go when it comes to requesting or receiving funding for your business. What venture you go will heavily depends on what you are trying to accomplish, and what amount of funds you need.

Below you will find a list of the various funding sources available to you as a business owner.

Loans

Loans are a simple form of funding. Acquiring a loan simply requires you to apply for one through your bank. Getting a loan can be one of the most straightforward methods, but it may not always be the most reasonable route for all people. Banks tend to have higher interest fees on their loans, and as well, as the loan can occasionally be harder to receive. If you do not have an optimal credit score, you may not be able to receive a loan through the bank. However, if you do, banks can sometimes be the easiest source to go through.

Online Lenders

Online lenders are growing in popularity, and are a great alternative to business loans through the bank. Many different online lenders are willing to lend to the majority of people. Simply go online, choose the one that best suits your needs, complete the application, and wait for a response. Depending on what online lender you look at, you may receive your response instantaneously. Otherwise, you will receive it within a matter of days. Online lenders are typically fast as well, issuing funds often within just a few days of applying.

Angel Investors

Angel investors are individuals who help start-up companies on a regular basis. The typical agreement when receiving investments from an angel investor is that they receive 20-25% return on their investment. One great aspect of having an angel investor on your team is that they are typically highly experienced with start-up businesses, and they can bring a unique skill set to the table to help you advance your company quicker. If you choose one properly, they may become both a financial asset to your business, as well as a skills-and-knowledge-based asset, too.

Venture Capitalists

Venture capitalists are similar to angel investors, except that they have no desire to be involved in the business itself. They will provide you with the investment funds, granted they agree to invest in the first place, and then they will expect you to continue with business as usual. It is a more hands-off approach to having investors. However, something to consider is that venture capitalists do still have a percentage in your company as long as you have their investment, so they can speak up whenever they desire, and based on the percentage of the company they currently hold, can have a significant influence on your business. For this reason, it is important to ensure that you choose an investor who will align with your business goals and needs, and whom you can trust.

Crowdfunding

There are many crowdfunding websites out there these days that allow start-up businesses to access funds by having a multitude of people make small investments toward the overall goal. Generally, someone will invest in a "tier" that you have created and based on which tier they invested on, they receive some form of gratuity back. So, for example, say someone invests at your top tier for $1,000. You might give them back a free product or service in return. In general, the investors are getting something as a "thank you" for investing in your company.

It is important that if you choose to use a crowdfunding website that you read the fine print. Many of these websites have specific rules about how much you can raise, the amount you must pay to the crowdfunding website host, and other details. For example, some require you to raise the full amount of your goal in order to keep the money, otherwise, they refund your investors. Be sure to pay attention to this so that you are clear on what needs to happen in order for you to successfully receive and access the funds that you need.

Grants

Many businesses are eligible to receive grants from the government. Small business grants enable small businesses to receive funds for fitting into a certain sector of the economy. Essentially, as a small business owner, you gain access to these funds for fulfilling a role in the overall economy. Each locale has a different selection of grants available to them, as does each industry, and sometimes even each niche. It is important to check into what these are for your own locale so that you can access any grants that may be available to you!

Chapter 11: Choosing Your Funding Source

If you do need funding, you are likely wondering what route you should go. In this chapter, we are going to explore how you can determine which funding method is likely the best option for you. This will ensure that you choose the method that will provide you with the capital, but that will take as little of your ownership away as possible.

How Much Do You Need?

The first thing that you need to consider when it comes to choosing your funding source is to consider how much you need. Certain sources are able to provide an ample amount, whereas others may not be able to. For example, crowdfunding is a great route if you need $15,000 or less, but is likely a poor choice if you need $50,000+. This is because it would simply take too many investors and too much time to get to where you want to go. That doesn't mean it can't be done. Instead, it means it may not be the most effective and viable option for you. Additionally, depending on what you are promising at each investment level, it may be unreasonable for you to fulfill that many smaller agreements as opposed to choosing a more direct and simple-to-fulfill option.

When it comes to considering how much you need, one thing to pay attention to is how much each source is willing to give you. For example, you may be most interested in the simple system of the bank loan, but the bank may not be willing to give you the full amount of what you require. You could always choose multiple funding sources at that point, but this would take away from the simplicity of it. In general, it is a good idea to try and limit the number of funding sources you access so that everything stays clean and clear. As well, most investors will be less likely to invest in someone who is significantly in debt with banks as this can make them a larger liability.

How Your Choice Affects Your Business

Your choice of where you choose to get your funding from affects your business in many ways. It can affect everything from how much debt you go into, to how much of your company you maintain ownership over after all is said and done. It is important that you make choices that are going to positively affect your company to the best of your ability. This doesn't mean that going into debt or bringing investors on for a share of your company is a bad thing. It simply means that there are certain circumstances where these tradeoffs do not make sense in relation to what you are looking for.

Consider what you are willing to risk for your businesses success. Sometimes, choosing to stay in a more conservative funding option that does not require you to carry such significant interest rates, or one that does not require you to give away shares in your company is more reasonable. Other times, the interest rates and the shares in the company are worth it for the value it will bring to your business. Alternatively, you may feel that bringing in someone like an angel investor, who has a somewhat high-interest rate and who will want a share of the company, is valuable because it also means you are bringing an expert to the table. What you choose is ultimately up to you, but consider how your choice will impact your company. One mistake many start-up companies make is selling off shares in the company too early in exchange for start-up capital. Doing this without effective strategies in place can quickly result in you losing majority share in your company, resulting in ownership ultimately being taken from you.

Consider Your Legal Structure

Another thing to consider is your legal structure. Certain legal structures are not eligible for certain loan methods. For example, sole proprietorships cannot seek investors because there is no official business entity for them to have a share in. For that reason, you need to consider which options are available to you with your chosen legal structure. This will ensure that you do not waste your time attempting to pursue a route that was never available to you in the first place.

Working Your Way up The Funding Scale

The best way to approach investing is to work your way up the funding scale. The funding scale works like this: at the bottom of the scale (where you want to start) consists of all of the least-risky options for lending. This would include receiving grants and crowdfunding. These two funding methods are great for raising capital without selling shares in your company or being required to pay it back. While you do typically have to fulfill some form of gratuity guarantee for your crowdfunding investors, you are not required to pay them back. This means that, financially, you are not indebted to anyone.

The next step up the scale would include slightly riskier options. These are options that include interest rates and fixed payments, but that does not include you selling any of your business shares. This would include bank loans and online lending. Here, you are receiving funds to grow your business, but you are not selling off any of your business to receive the funds. This means that even though you are in debt, you (and your partners, if applicable) are still in full ownership of the company.

The last step on the scale is the riskiest options. These are the ones where you are indebted *and* you have given shares of the company to receive your funds. For example, bringing in another partner with funds to invest, angel investors, venture capitalists, or otherwise gaining investors who will want their money back *and* want a share in the company in the meantime. These result in you giving away the most as an opportunity to create the funds needed for your business. As a result, they are the riskiest. These should be the last options you choose.

Again, which route you choose is ultimately up to you. However, you must ensure that it fits your financial needs, works with your legal structure, and results in you gaining the best-case scenario for your business. Do not make the mistake of taking risky moves without any form of strategy to protect yourself and your company. Whenever possible, always make the least-risky choice that you can, which will still bring in the guarantee that you need.

Chapter 12: Long-Term Finances

Most start-up companies think about their finances up until anywhere between the 6 - 12-month mark of business. In fact, many make the mistake of saving up 6 months of best-case-scenario funds and nothing further. This means they have no cushion or backup plan, resulting in many of them hitting a financial crisis early on in their business.

It is important that you have a cushion, but also that you have your long-term funds considered. Building a business takes time, and it is likely that you are not planning on only running your business for the next 6 months. For that reason, you need to consider your long-term finances.

First off, consider where your funds are coming from. If you intend on having all of your funds coming in through revenue, you will need to ensure that you are generating enough revenue to actually carry your business long-term. Otherwise, you need to consider your options.

The most common way to carry your business early on is either through working a job elsewhere while you are building your business, or bringing in investors. Working a job elsewhere in the meantime means that you have plenty of funds to continue to live your life and to invest in your business and build it over time.

However, it may not be the most reasonable option depending on the scale of your business, your financial needs, and what you are attempting to achieve. In that case, it may be time to start considering investors. Investors, under the right conditions, can provide you with enough capital to carry your business for quite a long time. This means that you will not have to worry about your finances in your business for quite some time.

One other option many people do not consider, and that is only truly available to certain types of entrepreneurs, is to have a subscription-based crowdfunding source turned on for your business. Companies such as Patreon allow entrepreneurs to encourage their fans to donate a certain amount of money per month toward the company, and they often receive some form of gratuity in exchange. This is the same as crowdfunding for start-up, except that pledges are made on a subscription basis, which means they continue to come in each month. Although this may not always generate a large amount of cash, some people have had great success with it, and it can become a reliable source of additional income for any start-up company to use.

Ultimately, you need to consider what your long-term financial needs are and generate a plan to get there. This comes through having a plan regarding where your finances are coming from, but it also comes with knowing how to manage your finances effectively. You will learn more about managing your finances to ensure the well-being of your business in Chapter 15.

Part Four: Administration Tips

Chapter 13: Bookkeeping

Bookkeeping is an essential, yet sometimes confusing part of the business. This is especially true for new businesses. Mature businesses typically have the luxury of hiring an official bookkeeper, but as a start-up, it is likely easier for you to learn how to do this yourself so that you can allot finances to more growth-focused areas of your business.

In this chapter, we are going to explore what you need to do in order to keep your bookkeeping duties simple yet efficient. This will be extremely helpful when it comes to managing accounts, overlooking cash flow, paying taxes, and more. Even if you don't necessarily want to, make sure that you start this immediately. This will save you from being disorganized and frustrated later on.

Keep Your Business and Personal Finances Separate

If you are running a sole proprietorship, or are running an LLC by yourself, it may seem like the easiest solution is to run your accounts together. The truth is, this is actually not effective and not ideal.

One major thing here is that when it comes to tax season, your tax auditor can audit both you and your business if you keep your finances together. This can be extremely frustrating for everyone involved. So, the better choice is to keep them separate from the very beginning. Treat your business as its own entity, even if it technically is not one.

A great way to keep them separate is to have your payments go into a bank account made specifically for your business. Then, you can have your business pay you on set days each month, just like a regular paycheck. Your business can then be run on the remaining funds. This way you are paid first and you receive funds, but everything is being operated effectively and separately.

File Your Tax Compliance Reports on Time

If you do not file your taxes on time, you can end up paying some major penalties. Even if you will not be able to pay the entire balance owing right away, you need to make sure you are on time. This can end up costing you big money if you aren't.

A great way to manage your tax funds is to have a separate account open and to automatically transfer a certain amount into that account every time your business receives money. This way, you have all of the funds you need to pay your taxes when tax season rolls around.

Keep Organized

There is nothing worse than having your bookkeeping systems messy and not being able to find what you need. Should you get audited or otherwise need to have access to certain information, not being able to locate it can result in serious penalties. You want to make sure that you are filing on time, and that everything is kept organized. Not only will this make taxes themselves easier, but it will also make managing and monitoring your money, overseeing your accounts, etc., easier to stay on top of.

A great way to keep things organized is to start by having an effective method that you will use to handle all of the paperwork that comes through. Most people will use a basic filing system that keeps everything organized by purpose, category, and otherwise. Pick a system that works for you and stick to it. This will ensure that you know exactly where to look to find everything that you need.

You should also enter your bookkeeping data in batches. Have a set date each month or week where all of your information is inputted into an online organizational platform. This way you have the hard copies available in your paperwork filing, but you also have everything backed up and organized online, too.

Another thing you need to do is continually pay attention to managing your cash flow. You want to stay on top of where money is coming from, and where it is going. Doing this will ensure that you are clear on what you are spending and what you are receiving. Regularly overlooking this can also ensure that if you are wasting or overspending in any particular area, you can correct this issue immediately and protect yourself from unnecessary financial loss.

Lastly, you need to review your bank statement and financial reports on a monthly basis. This will ensure that everything you have stored in your bookkeeping records is accurate and that nothing has been missed. It is a lot easier to catch a potential mistake right away and correct it than it is to wait several months and have no idea where the mistake was made, or what it was. As well, in many cases, if you wait too long, it cannot be corrected. Staying on top of this will keep everything organized and accurate.

Audit-Proof Your Records

In the event that you are audited, you will want to make sure that you have everything available for the auditors. For that reason, it is better to audit-proof your own records. Or, audit yourself. When you do this, you will ensure that anything an auditor may ask for or need to see is readily available for you.

To audit-proof yourself and your records, you need to make sure that you keep all of your debit and credit receipts. Any time you receive one, no matter how small the receipt is, keep it and file it under the category it belongs to. This way, if anyone ever needs them, you have them available and organized.

You should also ensure that you deposit all of your business cash flowing into the business. This will ensure that you are able to prove what is taxable (income) and what is not taxable (loans). This is a part of ensuring that you are not going to seem as though you are evading taxes for any given reason, or otherwise wrongfully structuring your tax returns.

Whenever Possible, Don't Go Into Debt

Lastly, the best thing that you can do is run your business on any cash that is already coming into your business. If you do not have enough funds to cover all of your expenses, the first thing you should do is consider how expenses can be cut. A great idea is also to ensure that you do not offer credit or otherwise to your customers, as you are not a bank and this is not your responsibility.

Whenever you can avoid going into debt, do so. Going into debt can make bookkeeping a lot more challenging. The more straightforward you can keep it, especially when you are newer and are unsure as to exactly what you are doing, the easier it will be for you to use this system.

Chapter 14: Budgeting

Setting up a budget for your business is a necessity. Even large corporations have budgets. Budgets are simply smart. They keep you on track, ensure that you are clear on what funds are being distributed and where, and allow for you to accommodate all of the expenses that go into running your business.

Even when you first launch your business, you should have a budget. Not only is this smart for you, but if you do decide to go with investors, they will want to see your budget as well. Keeping your budget simple yet effective is the best way to ensure that your funds will be adequately used. This also makes it easier for you to ensure that you have enough to actually cover the expenses of running your business.

Below are the steps you need to take to create an effective business budget.

Understand Budgeting Basics

Budgets are a necessary tool for businesses. It is important to understand how a budget works in business, as it is quite different from how a personal budget operates. Often, personal budgets come with a sustainable income that does not change too much. This means that your budget stays fairly fixed. However, when it comes to business, you generally intend on creating more sales on a monthly, quarterly, and yearly basis. For that reason, you need to understand how your business budget is unique.

A budget that is created for a business will accommodate anticipated revenues. These revenues are generally calculated on the previous year (and up to about three years) in business. However, since you are just starting out, you will need to generate your calculations based on market research. This will be your best-educated guess, and should likely be conservative to refrain from overestimating and not quite reaching your expectations. It is better to underestimate what you will make and come out with more than it is to overestimate and realize less.

Familiarize Yourself with the Three Components: Sales, Total Costs, Profits

The next thing you need to do is familiarize yourself with the three primary components in a business budget. These include sales, total costs (or expenses), and profits. These are the three numbers you are primarily focusing on in your budget.

Here is the importance of each of these components and what you need to know about them:

Sales

The sales number is generated by the amount of money your business makes. This includes all revenue streams, not just any particular level of sales. Any money coming into your business should go here. You should include your current position, as well as a forecast for your future projections. You will learn more about forecasting in a later section.

Total Costs

Your total costs account for all of the costs involved in the running of your business. This includes your overhead and everything you spend to actually get the sales coming into your business. You should include your fixed costs, such as rent, your variable costs, such as the cost of materials needed to make your products, and the semi-variable costs, such as the salaries of your employees.

Profits

Profit is the number you are left with when you calculate your revenue minus total costs. Profit is generally the goal of your business, so you want to ensure that your total costs are low enough that there is actually a profit to be had. This ensures that you earn a decent return on your investment.

Forecast Your Revenue

Forecasting what your revenue is going to be in future months, quarters, and years takes some practice. Since you are likely brand new in business, or within your first year, there is a good chance that you do not already have a strong enough volume of existing revenue to help you generate a number that is accurate for your business. This means you are going to have to research what other young businesses in your industry are accomplishing and estimate what a reasonable number would be for you.

Remember, since this is a prediction or projection method and not set-in-stone, forecasts are rarely accurate. Instead, they simply provide a guideline for what to expect when it comes to running your business. This forecast will give you goals, milestones, and direction, but will likely need to be adjusted along the way to represent what is actually going on in your business at the time.

The best way to forecast effectively is to be conservative. Remember, it is better to expect lesser results and achieve higher ones than it is to expect higher results and achieve lesser ones. You should assume that your sales volume will be lower and that your total costs may be higher. This ensures that you are conservative and hedged against unexpected expenses or circumstances.

Create a Spreadsheet

Once you are ready to begin, you'll want to start by having a spreadsheet. There are many templates you can use online, which may be the best way to start if you are new to budgeting. Otherwise, you can set up a spreadsheet for yourself. Again, if you choose to create your own, the best way is to use an existing template and adjust it as needed.

Determine the Details

With your spreadsheet ready, it is time to start putting together your budget! Begin with your fixed costs. Again, this includes anything that you must pay for every single month that is set at a fixed expense. Start here, because these are the ones where you know exactly what they cost, exactly when they will come due, and are easy to predict.

Next, you'll need to estimate what your variable costs will be and place them into your budget. This includes anything that will shift from month to month, depending on what your monthly business activities are. For example, if you sell products, you will have higher variable costs in months where you sell more products. Therefore, if you are anticipating selling more products in any given month, you will need to adjust the volume of these expenses accordingly. These are the expenses that cannot be accurately predicted, especially when you are new in business. Add these into your budget.

Lastly, estimate what your semi-variable costs are going to be. These expenses are generally a fixed component, but certain things can result in them changing. For example, say you pay an employee a salaried wage but you determine that they are going to get a raise or a bonus. This would make it a variable cost because it does change over time, even if not too terribly much. Add these into your spreadsheet.

The last part you need to account for is your goal for earnings. You do this by creating a desired profit margin. So, say your desired profit margin is 10%. Your goal would be to make 10% more than your business will be spending to ensure that you actually generate a profit each month.

Budget for Unexpected Expenses

Unexpected expenses are a natural part of the business. They happen all the time. Something unforeseen may occur, or an unexpected accident may happen, and before you know it there are more expenses that are required. This is especially true in new businesses. Since you are new to your business, you likely do not know exactly what it will take for you to run it. You might have an idea, but you may not be entirely clear on all of the costs surrounding this idea. Furthermore, you may decide at some point that you need assistance or want to hire help to get things moving along.

Having funds set aside for unexpected expenses is the best way to protect yourself and your business. This will prevent you from eating into your other expenses or having to cut your budget in many different ways to make up for the unexpected. A good rule of thumb is to set aside a certain amount of funds in a savings account for your business each month. This will ensure that you are able to afford anything that may arise unexpectedly.

Chapter 15: Cash flow

As a new business, you may not be entirely sure what to expect for your incoming and outgoing expenses. These can change drastically over time, and can also be challenging to produce when you do not have existing data already available from previous sales and cash flow. In this chapter, you are going to learn about how you can manage cash flow in your new business easily.

Know When You Will Break Even

It is important that you have a strong idea as to when you are going to break even in your business. This means the point at which your income will meet the same value as your expenses. Use this as your goal and create milestones to help you reach this goal. This ensures that your business will not be running too long in the red.

Monitor Your Cash flow Management Regularly

It is important that you monitor your cash flow effectively. In the beginning, especially, you need to refrain from focusing too much on your profits. While you do need to keep these in mind, using these as milestones will make it feel like you are forever failing at what you are trying to accomplish. Instead, focus on using these as your goals and create milestones to help you get there. Pay attention to passing these milestones, and the goals will be fulfilled naturally.

The more regularly you monitor your cash flow, the more you will be able to determine where your strengths and weaknesses are and what you can do to better achieve your milestones. You should make a habit of checking on your cash flow on a weekly basis to ensure that you are successfully moving forward. This will also help you catch any weaknesses, mistakes, or other potentially detrimental situations immediately, rather than waiting and catching them far too late.

Maintain a Cash Reserve

No matter how incredible your plan is, you are going to have expenses come up that were unexpected. Just as we talked about in budgeting, you need to have a strong cash reserve available in case anything comes up that requires additional funds. Keeping your cash reserves full and accessible for times when your business is not generating as much cash as it normally does, or when unexpected expenses arise is invaluable. This means that you will be able to afford these expenses in cash, rather than having to go into debt to make up for it. Whenever possible, you want to do everything in cash. This can be a major lifesaver for your business in the long run, especially in new businesses.

Look for Opportunities to Optimize Cashflow Management

It is generally not a great idea to manage the cash in your own business unless you absolutely have to. Having an accountant on hand can make it a lot easier, and also ensures that your management is optimal. However, since you are just starting out it is likely that you are going to have to manage your own cash flow for a while. For that reason, you need to regularly look for opportunities to optimize your cash flow.

The best way to simplify this is generally to use an online or digital platform that is known for helping to manage cash flow. There are many digital platforms which you can use that will allow you to input your budget, monitor incoming expenses, and keep everything organized and manageable. Using one of these can help optimize your cash flow management big-time!

Collect Receivables Immediately

Whenever you make an invoice, make it "due immediately." Ensure that you have net terms on it that limit it to being paid within 15 days or less. Ensuring that your receivables are paid immediately means that you are not chasing after people for money. Early on in business, many entrepreneurs make the mistake of making things too lenient for their clients. As a result, many get taken advantage of. As well, it is money you can rely on in value, but not in timing. This puts it as a disadvantage to your company.

Offer Discounts for Earlier Payments

A great way to ensure that your clients pay sooner is to have discounts for those who pay in full or who pay right away. You can also include in the net terms that there will be penalties for those who pay later. This usually encourages people to pay sooner, but also means that you are protected if they do not. Considering these parts of the service agreement can greatly protect your own earnings in your business.

Extend Payables When You Can

Although you want your receivables to be received as soon as possible, it is a good idea to set up your payables with as long of a payment period as possible. This means that, in the event that you do not have the cash to pay immediately, you have some extra time to sort it out. Doing this is a great way to hedge your business against those tough months and make the start-up process easier – without going into unnecessary debt.

Only Spend on Essentials

One thing you really need to ensure, especially when you are starting out, is that you are only spending money on things that are essential to your business. Something that tends to happen often when people are starting out is that they try to apply all of the bells and whistles of a mature company to their brand-new company. As a result, they end up spending far more than they need to. Focus only on what you must spend *right now* to acquire and maintain clients, and keep it at that. Refrain from having any unnecessary expenses. Only add more when they become necessary and when it makes sense to the growth and scaling of your business.

Be Conservative When Hiring

When you are hiring people, be conservative. Refrain from hiring anyone unnecessarily, particularly when you are first starting out. This will ensure that you are not spending money on salaries that could otherwise be saved or spent on something more valuable to the business. This is not only true for start-ups, though. This is true for any business. Be cautious about whom you are hiring and why. You should only hire those who will be an asset to your business, and only when that exact type of asset is truly needed to scale or grow your business further.

Use Your Technology Wisely

Technology is extremely helpful in the management of cash flow. Pay attention to using your digital cash flow management system and make the most out of it. Also, make sure that you are regularly backing up your data and that it is protected against potential file corruption or data loss or theft. This will ensure that you can easily access it and that you are not worried about the possibility of it disappearing at any given moment.

Chapter 16: Taxes

Paying taxes is a reality for any business and individual. As a business owner, how you pay taxes will differ from how you pay taxes on your personal income. In this section, we are going to discuss what you need to know and what you need to look into in order to ensure that you are covering yourself appropriately for your business taxes.

What Taxes Do I Pay?

The taxes you pay in your business heavily depend on what location you are in and what taxes are required to be paid for your legal structure. The best way to ensure that you are covering all of your tax expenses is to speak to an accountant and receive some information. Many small business accountants will do a consultation with you to ensure that you are properly accounting for the taxes that you need to be paying.

The structure of taxes can be quite unique based on the legal structure of your business. For example, if you are selling products or services that are required to be taxed, you can (and should) acquire a tax account from your local government. Then, you can easily begin to charge taxes on top of your fees when you are selling your products or services.

Small businesses that are run as a sole proprietorship or as a general partnership are generally taxed through what is called the "self-employed income" tax system. This means that your business is an entity independent of you. However, it is responsible for how your income is earned. These tax slips enable you to include your business earnings and expenses to decide your total taxable income.

Larger businesses that run using a corporate structure will generally benefit from having a specific accountant hired to help them with this process. Because there can be so many elements to filing taxes, you want to make sure that you have a skilled eye helping you to ensure nothing is missed.

How Much Should I Save?

Each locale charges a different amount of taxes per income bracket. The best way to ensure that you are going to have enough cash saved up by the end of the year to pay your taxes, is to save 20-25% of your overall earnings. That way, you can ensure that you will have plenty come year-end to afford the tax fees that you will incur.

Another idea is to consider signing up to do quarterly tax remittances. Tax remittances allow you to pay your taxes quarterly instead of annually. Taxes are paid based on what tax bracket you expect to be in by the end of the tax year. This means that if you overpay you may receive a refund at the end of the year. Alternatively, if you end up underpaying, you are still able to easily make up for it by the end of the year and you won't have such a large tax amount owing in the end.

Should I Hire An Accountant?

Many entrepreneurs, especially early on, wonder if they should hire an accountant when it comes to taxes. While your business is likely small enough that you do not need a year-round accountant, hiring one specifically for tax season and to offer periodic consults throughout the year can be extremely beneficial. However, it is completely up to you whether or not you want to do this.

Many small business owners successfully file their own taxes each year. The primary area where value is brought to the table by an accountant is when you have access to someone who is trained and knows what they are doing. This means it takes a lot less time, you can be sure that they are done correctly, and that you are receiving all of the benefits, breaks, and grants where applicable.

While the choice is ultimately yours, it is regularly recommended that business owners hire an account to at least help during tax season. Having this trained support can be highly beneficial and can ensure that everything is done appropriately.

Part Five: Branding and Marketing

Chapter 17: What Makes a Brand?

Branding and marketing your business is an essential part of running any business. As we move into the discussion of branding and marketing, we get away from all legalities and begin to focus on what is generally considered to be the more fun part of business! Here, you are going to learn how you can develop your own brand. Your brand is essentially the "image" of your business. It is what personifies it and gives it a true feeling, allowing your customers to feel like they are interacting with a sentient being instead of just a cash cow.

Your brand is where you get to be creative. You can bring your business to life, create an image for it, and really make it a lot of fun. Here you get to bring your vision into a reality and express that vision to your clients. Branding is extremely important. So, let's take a look at what makes a brand!

Knowledge of Target Audience

Strong brands have a powerful understanding of who their audience is. They know the exact demographic of who they are targeting, and as a result, they are able to create a powerful brand experience that appeals to their audience. Knowing your audience prevents you from attempting to create a brand that appeals to everyone. Since this is virtually impossible, unless you have a massive corporate brand like Walmart or Amazon, you are going to need to have a clear focus on who you are creating for.

Authenticity

Brand identities require authenticity. Attempting to create another run-of-the-mill brand image that has already been done a thousand times over will result in you not being seen or experienced by your target audience. To put it simply, you bore them. Instead, you need to identify and understand why your brand is so different from other brands out there and what it is about you that attracts your audience to you. Keeping your brand authentic and unique means that you will stand apart from the rest of the crowd. It also ensures that you will be memorable, capturing and staying in the minds of your target audience long after they actually interact with your brand.

Passion

Brands that have a passion for what they are doing end up being the brands that succeed the most. People love a brand that is personified. They want to emotionally resonate with the brands they love on a deep and intimate level. By interacting with your audience through effective, passionate branding, you make it a lot easier for them to fall in love with you and enjoy your brand experience.

Consistency

If you expect to receive repeat sales and to keep your business afloat and with a positive reputation, you need to take advantage of the power of consistency in your business. Consistency allows you to ensure that your customers receive the same phenomenal experience every time they interact with your brand. As a result, they begin to recognize you as a brand that is reliable, high quality, and enjoyable to interact with. Make sure to create a high-quality customer experience that you can easily repeat every single time, so that your customers always enjoy interacting with your brand.

Competitiveness

As we move forward with the digital age, and becoming an entrepreneur gets easier, more and more people are entering the business world. This means many different brands are being developed and shared with your target audience on a regular basis. As a result, you need to consider your competitiveness. Competitiveness plays a large role in making your brand stand apart and developing one that is worth pursuing. If you want your audience to recognize you and not your competitor, you need to be ready to take on the role of being at the top of the food chain. Prepare yourself by being willing to be a mover and shaker and by doing things differently.

Exposure

Exposure refers to the amount of viewing time your audience spends interacting with your brand. The more you are viewed by others, the better. This means that your audience grows rapidly because you are taking full advantage of getting in front of as many different eyes as possible. Using the internet, even extremely small companies with minimal budgets have the capacity to be seen by thousands, if not tens and hundreds of thousands of new eyes, on a monthly basis. Pay attention to your exposure and do whatever you can within your means to maximize the number of people with their eyes on you.

Leadership

Virtually every brand has a particularly influential leader behind it. In a large company, this individual tends to be the CEO. In a smaller company, it will be the owner—otherwise known as *you*. It is important that you are a strong leader for your brand and that you provide a positive influence on your team. Being the leader means that you are able to stay focused and on track. This means that your entire brand will stay focused and on track. Everything should pass through you first, before reaching the eyes of anyone else. This will ensure that you are able to qualify everything that contributes to your branding as something that supports your company in its growth.

Chapter 18: Building a Long-Term Brand

Branding is not a one-and-done thing. Although a lot of effort goes into creating the initial groundwork for a brand, an overall brand tends to become a living entity. With all of the moving parts and elements to the brand, it is easy to see why your audience will develop a relationship with your brand as long as it is created effectively. It is important that you understand how you can create a brand that will last long-term. In this chapter, we are going to explore what is involved in creating a lifelong brand that your audience will grow to know and love!

Keep Your Image Recognizable

A brand that is recognizable is one that has an easy time lasting through the ages. You want to make sure that your audience knows who you are and that you are recognizable to them. This means that your imagery, fonts, graphics, logos, colors, and other visual aids all need to remain consistent. You should also retain a consistent tone of voice behind your brand. Another great tool to use is a key phrase or tagline, which quickly enters the minds of anyone who thinks about your business.

Beyond these basics, however, you need to ensure that you keep your presence consistent and powerful. Building steadily and with integrity along the same recognizable pattern means that your audience will always know exactly who they are looking for.

Stay Flexible and Be Open to Evolution

Brands evolve over time. Remember, they do eventually become an entity and stand on their own. So naturally, just like a true being would, brands will evolve. The evolution is actually necessary. You want your brand to evolve with the times and stay relevant to all that is going on in the modern world. If you want to support the longevity of your brand, you have to make sure that you are allowing your brand to evolve.

The key to successful brand evolution is to ensure that the evolution is subtle and happens over time. A great example of this process is Coca-Cola. When people think of Coca-Cola, typically they think of a true red color, the classic white Coca-Cola logo, and the feel-good, relaxing energy that goes with their branding. In general, the image seems pretty consistent and solid. However, if you look through the history of Coca-Cola, there are some notable changes that took place over time. At one point, the brand colors, fonts, and logo even changed. It was as a result of consistent, subtle changes that they were able to evolve the brand to stay relevant and modern, without making such drastic changes that people were no longer able to recognize or identify the brand.

You need to incorporate this natural evolution process into your own brand, as well. This does not mean that early on you need to begin shifting and changing your brand. Instead, it means that as your company continues to remain intact and your brand continues to grow, you make subtle changes that make it more appealing to your growing audience and community of supporters. As a result, it grows even more enjoyable but does not, at any one point, become unrecognizable.

Maintain Your Purpose

Regardless of how your brand evolves over time, you need to ensure that your purpose for being in business remains the same. You do not want to operate with one single purpose and use this purpose to capture the hearts of your audience, only to flip the switch and completely change it. Especially not over and over again. Keeping your purpose clear, focused, and consistent ensures that your audience knows exactly what you are about and why you are in business.

You can also use your purpose to enhance their emotions and inspire them to follow you even more. For example, consider IKEA. This is a furniture company whose purpose is to "create a better everyday life." Their furniture is designed with the intention of making it easy to assemble, while being attractive and highly functional for their clients. They use this to enhance their client's emotional desire to have ease and functionality as a staple in their life. Often, they incorporate the emotions of their clients through showing them that this ease and functionality directly contributes to them having a more enjoyable family life. In their advertising you often see families gathering together and enjoying each other more, thanks to the time they have saved from having functional and attractive homes as a result of IKEA furniture.

Involve Your Employees

If you are a company that has employees, or when you do begin to incorporate employees into your company, always take the time to bring your employees into the branding process. Your employees likely interact with your audience a lot, maybe even more than you do. As a result, it is important to consult them when it comes to branding. This does not necessarily mean that they get the final say. However, including their input and listening to their inspiration is a great way to magnify the success of your brand.

Consider this: having several pairs of eyes focused on the success of your brand is powerful. This means having several different perspectives, insights, inspirations, and ideas to contribute to how you can evolve and expand your brand to become even more successful. You want to have several eyes on your brand, whenever possible. Your employees already work for you, and furthermore generally love being included in these types of processes. Incorporating your employees is a great way to enhance the quality of your brand and make it more appealing to your audience.

Enhance Customer Loyalty

Rewarding people who are loyal to your brand is a great way to maintain their loyalty and turn them into lifelong fans. If you want to have a long-lasting brand, you need to recognize who your biggest fans are and show them gratitude for the support that they have offered your company throughout the years.

The customers who are loyal to you are the ones who consistently go out of their way to share about you. They write to you, or write reviews about you, they share you with their friends and family, and they otherwise rave about how awesome you are to work with, or how incredible your company is. These individuals are sharing you a lot, which means you are receiving a lot of added business from them. Showing them thanks through exclusive rewards and perks is a great way to thank them for all that they do for you.

In some cases, simply offering a heartfelt thank you is enough. In other circumstances, you may prefer to make it a little more tangible and offer discounts or free swag to these fans. Giving your biggest fans the star treatment is a great way to show them that you are just as grateful for them as they are for you, which further expands brand loyalty. When people see this type of back-and-forth exchange taking place between companies, they become far more interested in what all of the love is about!

Be Aware of Your Competition

As with any aspect of your company, you need to be aware of your competition when it comes to your branding. Paying attention to what your competition is doing is a great way to enhance your own strategy, learn from their successes and mistakes, and catapult yourself into further success. Ultimately, you can use this awareness to tailor your brand to fill the gaps that other brands are not presently serving. The idea is to create a brand that appears and feels superior to the other brands out there. You want your customers to come to you, not to your competitor.

Chapter 19: Branded Marketing

Learning how to market, especially marketing on brand, is a special talent. It can take some time to really get the hang of it, especially if sharing and chatting about yourself and your awesome company is not something you are particularly used to. Even when we are wildly passionate about the company we are running, it can be easy to get stage fright or feel nervous when it comes to talking yourself and your brand up. For many of us, it just does not come naturally. In this chapter, we are going to explore how you can maximize your marketing efforts by staying on brand and taking a more comfortable yet still highly effective approach.

Sharing is Caring

One of the first things you need to learn about when it comes to modern marketing is the art of sharing. In the past, posting a cool picture of a happy model with your product in a public area was plenty to sell your products. These days, it is simply not enough. Your audience wants more from you. They *expect* more from you. Furthermore, if they don't receive it from you, they are going to wander straight into the arms of your competitor who is offering them exactly what they are looking for.

You need to focus on *sharing* your products, services, and brand with your audience. Showing is powerful, but it is nothing compared to sharing. In this day and age, people want to have an emotional attachment and personal connection to the brands they are purchasing from. They will quickly go elsewhere if they do not feel some level of relationship immediately growing between themselves and the brand of interest—*yours*.

The great news is: sharing is a lot easier than you might think. Rather than being a stuffy art of talking yourself up and "beefing up" the content, sharing is actually quite simple! All you really need to do is share content that is relevant to your brand. How this takes place will depend on whether you are running a personal brand or a separate brand with its own identity. You can learn more about each system below.

Personal Branding

If you are running a personal brand, you need to share aspects of your life that are relevant to your business. For example, say you are starting a company as a life coach who offers advice on relationships in particular. Share pictures of yourself on dates with your spouse, add small story updates to your social media profiles with short videos of you two enjoying time together and share small tidbits on how you are able to keep your relationship so fresh and successful. Sharing what it is that goes into your own success is a great way of showing how you can help contribute to other people experiencing similar success in their own relationships.

The key here is to make sure that these posts do not focus solely on you. Tell stories and give short informational updates with the intention of either inspiring or educating your audience. When you are aiming to inspire, it is okay to talk about yourself. However, you will want to leave your audience with a small lesson or a few words of wisdom that they can take away from the post. If you are aiming to educate, you can still share a story about yourself, but find a way to spin it and make it about them. A common way online marketers do this is by structuring a post like this: "Recently, I experienced _____. Have you experienced that, too? Were you _____..." Here, you are successfully creating relatability, sharing your own story, and making it all about your reader. It is both educational and personable.

Think about it this way: you don't sell yourself to potential friends or anyone else, do you? Not typically. That is generally why it is so uncomfortable: because it is not *natural*. Believe it or not, if it is uncomfortable for you, it is probably uncomfortable for your audience too. This means that it could end up being counterproductive.

A Branded Identity

If your brand is its own identity and has nothing to do with you, you need to share what is relevant to the brand. Share what your employees, clients, and other individuals involved in the brand are doing that is relevant to what your brand is all about. For example, if two of your employees go on a vacation paid for by the company and your brand is about freedom, ask them to share a few images of their trip online, and share those to your company pages. Choose to share content that highlights the purpose and values of your brand. The more you share, the more your audience will get a feel for what your brand is all about and why they should care.

80/20 Marketing Rule

Now that you understand how to share content, you are probably wondering how you can go about actual marketing. After all, sharing is a great method for exposure, but you do need to ensure that your audience knows that you have products or services for sale. They also need to know how they can go about purchasing them. That is where the 80/20 rule comes in. This is a marketing rule that teaches marketers to share 80% value and 20% sales pitches. This should generally be spread out over a week. So, if you share 1 post per day in a week, that is 7 posts per week. That means that of those posts, only one or two of these posts should include a sales pitch.

In that pitch, you want to make sure that you are intelligent about it. Share your story as you normally would, but include an opportunity to purchase a product or service from you. You can even design the story to be a sales pitch in and of itself, ending the post with their opportunity to purchase the product you have been sharing about in the rest of the post. Do not share too much about it, however. Highlight approximately three of the best aspects of the product or service, and encourage them to "learn more." Then, include a call to action in the post. This call to action is where they can actually go to learn more, whether that is messaging you directly or visiting your website.

When you distribute it evenly this way, people are more likely to engage with your brand and purchase from you. They become familiar with what you are selling, develop a relationship with you, and then go ahead and purchase. This is currently the structure that exists in the buyer's psychology, so taking advantage of this knowledge and using it for the growth of your business is powerful and important.

Staying On Brand

It is important that everything you do stays on brand. Whether you are sharing your personal brand or operating your brand as its own identity, keep everything organized and recognizable. Remember, staying recognizable is a major feature in being memorable, which is necessary if you want to experience repeat service. Staying on brand means that your tone of voice, imagery, fonts, colors, graphics, and all of the other visual aids involved in your branding all remain consistent in each post. This is true whether you are sharing a value post or a marketing post. If you choose to share other brand's content, news articles, or any content made by someone else, this content should also be on brand.

Fewer Expenses, More Efficiency

Lastly, as a new business owner, you need to consider the marketing expenses that you might incur. It may seem like a great idea to go out and spend a ton of money on paid advertisements and physical advertisements, but the truth is, this is actually extremely inefficient. In fact, it is quite wasteful of your finances, which are a precious resource especially early on.

The thing is, when you are first starting out, you don't know exactly who your target audience is. You may have a good idea, but you likely don't have an exact idea. As a result, you are going to struggle to create target advertisements or to know where to post or place your advertisements so that they actually get seen and generate a return on your investment. The better choice is to choose to use free or nearly free marketing strategies, to begin with. Social media posts, word of mouth, networking and other less expensive alternatives are a great way to get your name out there without spending a small fortune. Then, once you begin generating more money *and* a clear sense of who your audience is, you can expand into your paid advertisement options. That way, you know exactly where to place them and how to target them to reach your demographic and therefore experience the greatest results.

Part Six: Customers

Chapter 20: Your Customer Experience

Customers are an essential part of any business. Without them, you simply won't make any money! For that reason, it is important that you pay attention to your customer experience. Your customer experience is the experience your customers have when they interact with your brand. Through intention and regular monitoring, you can ensure that your customer experience is one that will have them eager to come back to you.

Focus a Lot on a Little

One of the best rules of thumb when starting out a business, is to focus on having a few primary points of your customer experience amplified. Rather than trying to attempt to have massive systems in place, ones that will likely become overwhelming and not produce a great return anyway; start smaller.

When you focus your efforts on two or three primary customer experiences, it allows you to really amplify the quality of these experiences. For example, say you have an online presence and you launch a free weekly or monthly podcast. This podcast should account for one of your three methods for creating a customer experience. By not stretching yourself too thin through overpromising, you ensure that your podcast can be successfully designed with massive value.

There are many ways that you can design a customer experience. Ideally, you should have about three parts of the experience that are free and contribute toward attracting new customers, and approximately three more that are a part of the paid experience and that are designed to amplify the paid experience. An example of part of your paid experience might include an exclusive downloadable offer just for your paying clients, or access to a VIP "club" such as a Facebook group or e-mail list that grants them access to exclusive content.

Make sure that you stay focused on these experiences and refrain from adding in too many at once. Perfect these ones, and later when you scale your business, you can focus on adding in more.

Be Deliberate

When it comes to building your customer experience, be deliberate. You want to make sure that you are very intentional about everything you are incorporating into the experience. This includes the very structures you choose, as well as the time and value you put into them. A great way to be deliberate is to consider the plans you have for your customer experience. Understand *why* you have incorporated certain elements. This will give you a clear focus and set of goals to ensure that each point of the experience is truly magical for your audience.

For example, imagine that you are a marketing agency. You choose to incorporate a free weekly podcast as a part of your customer experience. Consider every aspect of how this is going to serve your customers. What do you want them to gain from this podcast? How long will it take for them to consume it? What amount of time allows you to offer ample value, without giving away too much of your time and services? How can you use this as a point of interest to draw clients into your paid offers? Once you have considered these questions, you know exactly how much value you need to include, how to create and structure the podcasts, and what your marketing objectives are with them. Yes, you are creating them with the intention of offering free, valuable and usable marketing tips. However, you are also creating them to help potential clients get an idea of what you are all about and make the ultimate decision as to whether or not they want to work with you. Therefore, you are offering two important pieces of information. Include everything you can to help your clients feel as though they have received wonderful free value, but also to encourage them to purchase value from you.

Modify It As Needed

Once you have designed your customer experience and begun to build it, do not be afraid to modify it as needed. If you see windows of opportunity to amplify the experience and make it even more enjoyable for your customers, use this as inspiration and go ahead and make your adjustments!

A great way to monitor the experience is to pay attention to reviews and customer feedback. Then, as it comes in, pay attention to trends. If you see inspired ideas or any particular trends that show up as an opportunity for improvement, take advantage of it and implement them! This will make your customer experience far more enjoyable. Which as you know, means more customers in the long run.

Chapter 21: Keep Customers Coming Back

Getting customers to purchase from you is important, but keeping your customers is just as important! It tends to be a lot easier to encourage existing customers to purchase again than it is to get new customers to come in. That doesn't mean you should not focus on new customer acquisition, but it does mean that you also need to pay attention to existing customers. This all contributes to the consistent revenue that you earn from sales in your business.

Nurture Your Customer Relationships

The first way to ensure that customers come back is to nurture your relationships with them. This starts from the moment you acquire a new customer. Through consistent brand image and experience, your customers are shown "who" you are and what you are all about. From there, you can encourage loyalty by offering various rewards and encouragement to continue following you!

Sharing content is a great way. This is especially true when the content offers some form of tangible value that your audience can appreciate. As you might remember from the "Customer Loyalty" section, using strategies like offering free services, discounts, or swag to loyal customers is a terrific opportunity. However, you can go much further than that, too.

Consider making nurturing your audience and customers a regular thing. For example, if you have an exclusive online community or newsletter specifically for people who have purchased from you, include content that is only for their eyes. This may be free training, free e-books, free music playlist downloads, free upgrades on their next order, or otherwise. You can also spotlight customers in these areas. Show off the customers who are raving about you in a spotlight post or article in your newsletter and thank them for the appreciation. This shows your audience that you care and allows you to nurture your relationship with them.

Another massively underrated way of nurturing your audience is by including them in the process of your business. Your audience supports you, and naturally, they love being a part of what you are doing. Giving them "insider" opportunities or insight allows your audience to feel extra special. The key is to do this in a way that keeps you as the expert or leader but allows them to become involved. For example, allowing your audience to name your next product or service. Alternatively, you can involve them by sharing behind-the-scenes clips, images, and stories from your company or your life (depending on whether you are a company-based brand or a personal brand.) Allowing your audience to truly develop a relationship with your brand is a powerful way to nurture your relationship with them. Chances are, they already want to have a relationship with you. It is just up to you to provide them the access points to do that.

Invite Them Back

One effective way of getting repeat customers is actually pretty straightforward: invite them back. Sometimes, as life goes on, customers will forget about your brand. This is not because they did not thoroughly enjoy their experience with you. Rather, they may not have felt a need or urge to shop or work with you. As a result, they simply forget.

Using strategies like newsletters and other outreach systems to reach out to your audience and invite them back to your business. Catchy taglines like: "Hey, ____! I think you'll LOVE this new [product/service]!" or "Hey ____, we miss you! Here's a free [offer] just for you," are great to help remind them about you and invite them back to your business.

Depending on the structure and scale of your business, you can also personally reach out to previous customers and achieve the same results. For example, by reaching out and thanking them for their previous purchase and asking if there is any way that you can support them in the present. Or, if you sell products, letting them know about a new product that you think they might be interested in.

Chances are, if you take a moment to invite your customers back, and your brand experience was positive and your product or service was valuable, they will be more than happy to come back. That, or you will end up relevant in their mind again and they may just begin sharing you with more of their friends and family! Ultimately, as long as your invitation back is heartfelt and genuine, you cannot go wrong.

Part Seven: Scaling and Outsourcing

Chapter 22: When and How to Use Automation

Automation is a highly popularized tool for scaling businesses in the modern world, and for great reason. When it comes to scaling, automation is extremely powerful. However, there is a lot of false information going around about the purpose and use of scaling, and when, how, and why you should do it. In this chapter, we are going to explore this valuable tool and discover how it will benefit you and how you know it is the right time to start using it.

Why Waiting Is Better

Many get-rich-quick schemes out there advertise that starting and running a fully-automated business is the way to make money in your sleep right off the bat. Unfortunately, the only people who tend to get rich from these systems are those who are selling you the automated services. In the past, this may have worked, but in modern times, people want a relationship with the company they are purchasing from. Therefore, most fully automated businesses, especially ones that are brand new, tend to be overlooked and unappreciated by your target audience.

Instead of causing a gap in your relationship with your audience, you should consider waiting and not implementing automation until later on (see: "When to Start" below). Waiting gives you plenty of time to develop genuine, personalized connections with your audience. This means that they truly get to know who you are and what your brand is all about. Furthermore, it gives you the opportunity to create market research, where you begin to understand who your audience is, how they communicate, what they love about your business, and why they are actually interested in it.

When to Start

Knowing when to start automation is simple: you start when it will add massive value to your customer relationships. Keep in mind that automation tends to be considered "impersonal." Therefore, you need to build a highly personalized brand that is great at creating genuine relationships. Then, once you have done so, you can use these automation tools to amplify the value that you offer to your clients and further improve your relationships.

For example, say you spend the first six months of your business building relationships through personal connections. You network, offer free live training, input your inspired written content and so forth during this time. Then, at some point, you realize your relationships are growing and it is taking up far too much time for you to continue to nurture them exclusively in this way. So, instead of carrying on and putting too much on your plate and burning out, you begin to download some of your live training and automate them. You include them on a landing page with a sign-up link. This gives your audience the opportunity to establish a personal connection with you through email, and then also gives them access to the free live training. That way, they gain access to the added value that you have already given away for free. However, they also gain the opportunity to build a personal connection with you through your e-mail newsletter.

The only time you should truly implement automation is when you have scaled through personal interaction enough that it has become too much. When you no longer feel like you have adequate time to devote personal one-on-one attention, then you begin including automated content and sources. This way, you are still able to include some personalized content, but you are not strapped down to your computer 24/7 trying to keep up with all of the relationships you have created with your clients.

How Automation Will Benefit You

Once you are ready to begin automating your business, the benefit you gain is massive. It makes building and scaling your business significantly easier. Because you are able to automate things, you can create a single piece of content and use it several times over to establish new customer relationships and to provide added value to existing ones.

Another great automation tool is using automated post schedulers to post all of your content for you. Then, instead of having to jump on your computer or phone on a daily basis and upload new content, you can simply schedule it out for several days or even weeks in advance. This allows you to spend more time away from your computer and business creating more inspired content or enjoying your life, rather than feeling hung up having to personally be involved in every little detail.

Chapter 23: Outsourcing and Hiring

Eventually, in your business, you are going to want to outsource or hire someone. This is a natural part of scaling your business as you grow. This can also be a fairly daunting task to a new business owner who does not have a large amount of experience in this area of business. In case you have any questions about outsourcing and hiring, we are going to answer them in this chapter.

Outsourcing vs Hiring

The first thing you may be wondering is what the difference is between outsourcing and hiring, and why you should choose one versus the other. So, let's explore the differences and see when and why you might choose either option.

Outsourcing

Outsourcing is something you do when you enter a work agreement with someone, but you do not hire them as an employee of your company. Consultants and contractors are the two most common types of outsourcing agreements businesses enter. These agreements allow someone else to take on the responsibility of overseeing a certain task in your business, but without them becoming an official employee. This means you do not have to oversee training fees, salaries, and other expenses related to hiring an employee. Instead, you simply sign a work agreement with someone who is already in business for themselves and let them do their work.

You pay according to the agreement. This payment may require immediate payment, a retainer and then the final payment upon completion, or the complete payment upon completion. It highly depends on the agreement and the individual or business whom you have entered the agreement with. The most common payment method, however, is to pay a retainer and pay the remaining balance upon completion.

Hiring

Hiring someone is the process of bringing someone in as an official employee of your business. You hire them to work for you, then you take responsibility for training them, paying them a regular salary, and providing them with employee benefits that are generally necessary for the workplace. This may include but is not limited to benefits like health insurance, workers comp, unemployment insurance, and more. Upon choosing to hire someone, you would need to look into the legal requirements per your locale.

When and Why You Should Outsource

Outsourcing is typically the first form of "hiring" someone to help your business. Hiring a company or individual to perform certain tasks for you without you having to bring them in as an actual employee can be highly beneficial. This is highly cost-effective for most start-ups, and can also be done in a way where the service is not ongoing. In other words, you only pay when you need the support. Plus, you can go to websites like Fiverr or Upwork to explore the opportunity of outsourcing for a minimal fee. This makes outsourcing even more cost-effective and still yields great results.

The best time to begin outsourcing is when you can reasonably afford the service. As soon as you can, begin to outsource the parts of your business that you are the weakest at serving. That way, you can have an expert on board offsetting your weaknesses and amplifying the strength of your business. Then, you can focus on what you are truly great at!

When and Why You Should Hire

Unlike outsourcing, hiring someone requires an actual commitment. You are committing to pay the fees to train this individual, as well as to keep them on in your business. This means you will be paying a regular salary to this individual over the time that they work for you. While you can certainly hire for temporary roles, it will still cost you quite a bit to do it. When you decide it is time to hire someone, it should be because you truly need someone to fulfill a role on an ongoing basis and the cost of hiring them is equal to the value that they will bring to your business.

Make sure when you hire someone that you are in a stable place in your business and that hiring them makes sense financially. You do not want to commit to hiring someone, only to find yourself unable to pay their salary because your business is not generating a steady enough income.

Additionally, make sure that when you do hire someone, you choose to hire a person who is going to bring massive value to your business. Consider individuals whose strengths offset your weaknesses, and who are willing to devote themselves passionately to the success of your business. This does not necessarily mean they will be as devoted to your business as you will be, because that may be nearly impossible since it is *your* dream. However, they should be devoted to helping you experience success in your business.

As you hire more and more employees, make sure each hire is strategic and brings great value to your business. If they can amplify your success and help you scale through to your next level and every level after that, this makes them significantly more valuable. Refrain from hiring someone just because you are in desperate need of somebody to fill a spot in your company. This often results in you getting ineffective employees who may cost more than they are worth to your company. As well, look into your legal obligations as an employer to refrain from unnecessary lawsuits or otherwise.

Conclusion

Starting a business is a massive undertaking. As a new business owner, you are taking on a lot of roles and responsibilities at once. Especially in the very beginning, virtually everything that goes into running your business will fall on your own shoulders, and if applicable, your partners'. This means that you need to be prepared to handle all that comes with this commitment and educate yourself in every way possible.

While you don't need to make it more complicated than it already is, you do need to understand that it *is* a complicated task and it will require your devotion and commitment.

One wonderful thing about business, however, is that there is nothing more fulfilling than seeing a vision that you are deeply passionate about coming to life. As long as you have a strong strategy in place and the willingness to overcome any obstacle that lands in your path, you are sure to experience success in your entrepreneurial journey.

I hope that through reading this book you were able to learn plenty of information to help you get started on that path. From developing your idea to knowing how and when to scale it, I have done my best to include as much information in this book as I could to help you get started.

The next step is to consider where you are already at in your business and begin to grow from there. If you already have your vision, move forward in developing your plan and putting it into action. If you have your plan and have already begun taking action, I hope this book provided you with great tips and tools to verify and strengthen your plan and take your actions just that much further.

Lastly, if you enjoyed this book, I ask that you please take the time to review it on Amazon. Your honest feedback would be greatly appreciated.

Thank you.

Check out more books by Greg Shields

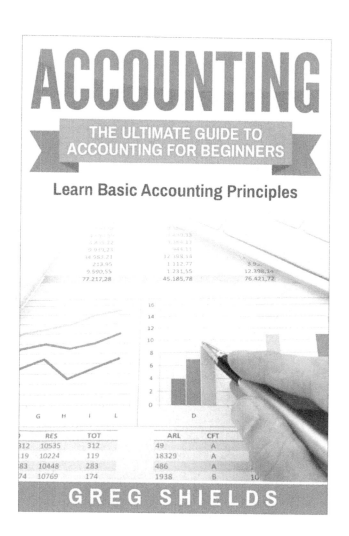

ACCOUNTING

THE ULTIMATE GUIDE TO ACCOUNTING FOR BEGINNERS

Learn Basic Accounting Principles

GREG SHIELDS

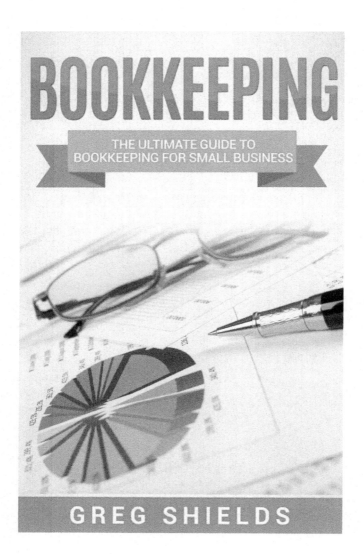

Made in the USA
Monee, IL
01 December 2020